GW00670459

Different Worlds:
A Virtual Journey

Different Worlds:
A Virtual Journey

Editor
Santosh Kumar

Contributing Editors
Marguerite Carstairs
Karunesh Kumar Agrawal

Publisher
Cyberwit.net
4/2 B, L.I.G. Govindpur Colony,
Allahabad-211004 (U.P.) India

Tel: (91) 09415091004
E-mail: cyberwit@rediffmail.com
www.cyberwit.net

ISBN 81-8253-064-4
First Edition: 2006
Rs. 650/-

This book was printed in India by Cyberwit.net

Aamer Fort, Jaipur, India

"There are no foreign lands. It is the traveller only who is foreign."

-Robert Louis Stevenson

"The whole object of travel is not to set foot on foreign land; it is at last to set foot on one's own country as a foreign land."

-G. K. Chesterton

"For my part, I travel not to go anywhere, but to go. I travel for travel's sake. The great affair is to move; to feel the needs and hitches of our life more nearly; to come down off this feather-bed of civilization, and find the globe granite underfoot and strewn with cutting flints."

-Robert Louis Stevenson

I always get that excited feeling that here is another place I have yet to see, when I sit down and buckle up in an airline seat, or a bus or most recently, the Korean KTX Train. Somehow looking at pictures, and then reading the story that accompanies the pictures, always sends me into another world.

The amazing thing is that when I am looking at the travel magazines, I am almost always travelling somewhere, and in a way, that is what is happening, I am travelling to a different place and maybe a different time, and reliving the journey and the experience, as I read and look at the photographs.

This book is going to take you on many different journeys through many different places in the world. Through the photographs here, you can experience what someone else has experienced, and feel the marvel or the awe, or the feeling they felt, when they focused on this particular scene, and also chose the image to put into this volume.

What makes a great image? I have been doing many reviews on an art review site lately, and what I realised is that, certain images have a part of the photographer's eye and soul in them. These are images that has inspired or moved the photographer, and the feeling or excitement is sometimes leaping out of the image, or flowing out to wrap around the viewer and entice them to feel and experience what the photographer saw.

Words cannot adequately describe what an image can portray so vividly. I also feel as an artist, that we convey what we feel about what we perceive, and that feeling, is what the viewer responds to. Great images absorb the viewer and bring them into the scene. Certain images have this inspirational quality that makes one want to stop and ponder, in the same way that we stop and ponder, when confronted with something inspirational or something moving.

It could be something as small and as delicate as a moss garden blown up with a macro, to show whole life shapes and living organisms, all existing within a miniscule world. It could be something as vast as an entire walled ancient city viewed from high up in a plane, or a whole mountain range.

Different Worlds exist in the reflection in a drop of dew, or the entire rainbow over the sea, in the eye of a tiger or the gaze of a young child or animal. There are many different worlds and there are many different interpretations of what is different, from the painting by the traditional artist, to the digital creation of the graphic designer.

Many who cannot travel, find their journeys through the images of other travellers. Even seasoned travellers sit and dream when confronted with an image of a location or world they may not have known even existed.

The Ice castles and hotels of Sweden and Harbin, fascinate and attract, as much as the coral reefs of the Australia's Barrier Reef, or the sunken wrecks of New Zealand's Stewart Island. The scenic countryside of the Australian Outback, and the Backwoods of America, vie against the frozen Niagara Falls and the Opulence of Los Vegas and the fast Life.

The sultry beauty of India, and the stark reality of The Great Wall of China, play against the azure waters of the Caribbean and the Greek islands, and the Castles of Europe and the temples of Asia hold much magic and mysticism, and take us to places we can never imagine existed.

Many of us live in a place we call home, and many of us may not even realise that what is usual to us, is a 'Different World' to someone living in another land. We may live in one place, and may never have travelled to another part of our own country. There are different worlds within different world,s and this is what this book is about. People share a slice of their different world, and the reader, travels with the photographs to many places beyond their realm of experience.

We can never say we have been there and seen it all, and done it all.

Here is a slice of life as seen through the eyes of different artists from many different places, and may the feeling that inspired the artist, come through to you and inspire you too, so you too can share and experience what the artist experienced.

Thank you to all the artists who shared their Different Worlds. You have made the life of all of us richer with your experience.

Marguerite Carstairs
http://M-carstairs.com/travel

Marguerite Carstairs, who creates under the Artist name of Ladymaggic, is a versatile and colourful artist who is a photographer, digital artist and Oil painter. She delights in sharing her experiences through her many websites, focusing on her different interests and experiences.

Her main focus is the unique beauty of both Nature, and what Man has

constructed, and she travels extensively following her interests and feelings. Every trip is an adventure, and every experience is an artwork. Her contribution here is based on what she considers to be the most wonderful recent thrills of her life. These are walking The Great Wall, Climbing Naejeonsan Mountain, and driving from Broome to Perth.

CONTENTS

Alan Morgan	113	Karen Pike	60
Alice Parris	114	Kari Korhonen	62
Andrew McIntyre	129	Karunesh Kumar Agrawal	13
Barbara Beck-Azar	17	Kym Lovell	64
Barbara Simcoe	19	L Lindall	65
Ben Albares	9	Lárus G	66
Bob Blackett	21	Linda Block	67
Cher Peterson	23	Louie Levy	14, 150
Cheri Carter	25	Marguerite Carstairs	69
Darlene M. Nixon	27	Marie Calow	72
David Miller	29	Maureen Audley	153
David T. Culver	31	Michael Estabrook	74, 121
Dawid Wiacek	32	Mike Howe	75
Debs Higginson	34	Mirsad Mehulic	77
Dennis Everett Newell	36	Patricia Fritsche	79, 123
Dominique Lecomte	38	Patricia Wellingham-Jones	80
Emily A. Reed	40	Pepita Selles	82
Eric Tessier	133	Phil Kunin	84
Erika Brodie	42	Rebecca L Phillips	86
Floriana Hall	115, 138	Robert L. Bills	88
Greg Edwards	44	Robin M Buehler	90, 127
Greg VandeVisser	46	Robert M. Wilson	124
Jan Kolling	47	Roger Cummiskey	92
Jan Oscar Hansen	117	Sam Stearman	101
Janet K. Brennan	49	Sandra Busby	94
Jean Ann Fitzhugh	52	Shari Travison	16, 96
JEM Wellen	53	Shirley Bolstok	97
Jennifer Johnson	54	Steven P. Love	99
Jeremy R Meier	12, 56	Tabitha L. Borges	104
Jerry Bradley	119	Tatiana Pahlen	105
Jim Corbett	57	Tazda Lawson	108
Jim Ganley	142	Trisha Allard	110
Joseph Ganley	58	Yvonne Sparkes	112, 128
Joseph Steven Valencia	59	**NOTES ON CONTRIBUTORS**	154

View from Aamer Fort, Jaipur, India

Ben Albares

Photo by Ben Albares www.benalbares.net

Málaga (Andalusia), artists' cradle, where the music gets paid it forms and the happiness invades its white streets and its people. The light turns its landscapes and evenings into a singular and unique place in the world.

Photo by Ben Albares   www.benalbares.net

Asturias, daughter of an ancestral culture, the Celtic ones. Patrimony of the time, because their streets and monuments they transport you to another time. And their music revives the memory of distant times. The respect for the nature has converted its virgin beaches and their green landscapes into a natural paradise.

Barcelona, mixture of cultures and art, a fantastic place to get lost in an artistic dream. Full with coloring and unique forms. It invites you to get lost for their corners full of surprises, cosmopolitan city where to meet new people it is an adventure.

Jeremy R Meier

Sony Center - 2000

Sony Center - 2000 - A complex snapshot of one of the largest structures within Potzdamer Platz, Germany. The photo itself is generated from a reflection of a reflection; the fountain water, skylight glass, and metallic structure combine for a striking high-contrast assembly.

Karunesh Kumar Agrawal

Photo of a Child Near Jal Mahal

Jal Mahal

An attempt to capture the beautiful moment of a playing child held by mother's hand.

Jal Mahal built in 1799 A.D. in the midst of a lake as a pleasure spot. The lake was formed by construcing a dam between the two hills. During the winter months we find a large number of migratory birds at the lake.

My visit to Jaipur in November 2005 inspired the creation of these photos.

Louie Levy

'Misty Dusk at Reflections'
Central Park Lake, NYC 1965

'Sunrise Ice Freeze'
Bayside Park, Queens, NYC 1975

Shari Travison

"Beyond the Trees" (Monterey, CA)

"Beyond the Trees" (Monterey, CA) - This graphite drawing was based on a photo taken in Monterey, California, located in Central California along the Pacific Ocean. The drawing is a small snapshot of the famous "17 Mile Drive" which consists of beautiful homes, plants, beaches, seal and bird rocks, and lush green golf courses one of which is the championship "Pebble Beach Golf Links". Monterey County has an expansive shoreline (approximately 100 miles long). The County also has many other places to visit including the Monterey Bay Aquarium, Cannery Row, Fisherman's Wharf, Historical gardens, and several comfortable lodgings including Hotels, Bed & Breakfast Inns, and Luxury Resorts.

Barbara Beck-Azar

ASIR Baskets

Bedoiun

ASIR Baskets - Watercolor, still life of Handwoven baskets from Khamis with a Turkish blanket... the baskets have camel skinned bottoms and are beautifully made.

Bedoiun Woman in solitude of the desert. the coverings worn aren't always bleak and in fact protect the delicate framework of woman and in that lies strength. I chose earth tones to show the oneness with the desert spaces...

Maui Palm

Searching for Truth

Maui Palm - Watercolor of palm from hotel room while in maui... this one moment on my balcony allowed the space to paint this beautiful palm... it's just a sketch -showing the light and airy environment of the tropical paradise we all know and love.

Searching for Truth -- painted in Khamis Mushayt KSA -- Watercolor image regarding man's search for through through written words, the world we live in and the often confusing messages out there. only in solitude may a man find the peace he searches for...

Barbara Simcoe

Avalon

Avalon - Original acrylic painting on canvas, framed, 28 x 22". Prints also available. This is probably THE most painted view of Avalon, the city on Catalina Island, off the coast of LA. This was done from a photo I took, while traveling by bus on the island.

Ballachulish

Cacti 'n Bloom

Ballachulish - Acrylic painting on canvas, 18 x 36", unframed, completed in 2001. This is one of my favorite images - a lakeside view, from a hotel in which I stayed, in Scotland, during a trip to Great Britain.

Cacti 'n Bloom – Acrylic painting on canvas, 18 x 24", unframed. Mate to "Desert 'n Bloom", both done in 2005, when Arizona and other soutwestern states had an extremely wet Spring, which generated tons of wildflowers – some unseen for over 100 years.

Desert 'n Bloom

Spider Rock

Desert 'n Bloom - Acrylic painting on canvas, 18 x 24", unframed. Mate to "Cacti 'n Bloom", both done in 2005, when Arizona and other soutwestern states had an extremely wet Spring, which generated tons of wildflowers – some unseen for over 100 years.

Spider Rock - Original acrylic painting on canvas, framed, 19 x 36". This is the famous Spider Rock, located at one end of Canyon de Chelley, in Arizona. It's a magical place and this rock is believed to be the cradle of the American Indian civilization by some of the tribes.

Bob Blackett

Reflection in Middle America

Reflection in Middle America - A small shop in Williamsport, Pennsylvania, USA. The items carried must reflect the tastes of the neighborhood, which is not rich or poor.

West Branch of the Susquehanna River

World's End State Park

West Branch of the Susquehanna River - The quiet on the river contrasts with its past, when it was the artery for the local lumber industry.

World's End State Park - The scene in World's End State Park in Pennsylvania, USA is spectacular. This area is less than three hours by car from New York City.

Cher Peterson

Death Valley from Above

Death Valley from Above was taken from the top of the Cottonwood Mountains of Death Valley National Park. A four-wheel drive, dirt road leads up to the top of the mountain range, providing unlimited vistas of Death Valley.

Desert Plants and Mountain Ranges

The Panamint Dunes

Desert Plants and Mountain Ranges   is an image taken from the Saline Ridges of Death Valley National Park. Again, you must be an adverturist with a sturdy 4-wheel drive vehicle to gain access to this view of the northwestern portions of Death Valley.

The Panamint Dunes are some of the most remote and beautiful of all the dunes found in Death Valley National Park. Found in the Panamint Valley, it is quite a hike through the desert to reach these dunes that have been utilized by Native Americans for many millinium.

Cheri Carter

650 Yamaha V Star

Skydiving

Maggi Carstairs has been after me to put a couple of my skydiving pictures in the running....here are two freefall pictures and one of my other passion, my 650 Yamaha V Star.

Darlene M. Nixon

Double Helix

"Double Helix" is an original oil painting on canvas of two Japanese snow cranes doing a premating dance reminding me of the doubling and dividing of the double helix of DNA stands. The canvas is roughly 24" x 36.

Homecoming

Lake Island

"Homecoming" is a depiction of a dragonfly hunting in the grasses of the Au Sable dunes which overlook the National Lakeshore of Lake Superior on the edge of the Upper Peninsula of Michigan. This also is an original oil painting on canvas measuring 18"w x 24"h.

"Lake Island" is a bird's eye view of cattails looking out across the water to an island in a small lake in Michigan's interior. It is an original oil painting on canvas measuring 12" x 24".

David Miller

Angkor Wat in Cambodia

Bagan, Myanmar

Yangon, Myanmar

Bagan, Myanmar - where a thousand Buddhist stupas cover the landscape.

Yangon, Myanmar, in a park near the 2 500 year old Shwedagon Pagoda.

David T. Culver

Railroad

Statue Picture

Dawid Wiacek

Jumping before the Torre de Oro in Seville, Spain

Sunset in Cadiz, Spain

Swan Swimming in
Sintra, Portugal

Debs Higginson

Approaching Ammanford

In the Welsh Valleys

Approaching Ammanford
Medium: Oil Paint - The view travelling through the mountains, leaving Swansea and approaching Ammanford.

In the Welsh Valleys
Medium: Oil Paint - The view from the road as you leave Craig Cefn Parc, Swansea.

Path to the Chateau

Path to the Chateau
Medium: Oil Paint - A Chateau in Southern France.

Dennis Everett Newell

The Elk pics from Benezette Mountain near St.Mary's, PA

Hamlin Beach State Park, Hamlin NY

Waters of Tampa Bay, Florida

The Dolphin Pic I took in the Waters of Tampa Bay, Florida... The Elk pics are from Benezette Mountain in near St.Mary's, PA.. and the two somewhat abstract pics I took near my home in Hamlin Beach State Park, Hamlin NY.

Dominique Lecomte

Bar

Le vélo vert

Les rocheuses

"Bar" is a photograph. One of many strange places you can see in Miami Beach, Florida, USA

"Le vélo vert" is a photograph. This bicycle was leaning along a wall near a church in Valladolid, Yucatan, Mexico and looked like it had been there for quite a while.

"Les rocheuses" is a hand colored woodcut, size 6x16", edition 8. A view of the mighty Rockies mountains somewhere in Colorado, USA

Les tentes rouges

New York, NY

"Les tentes rouges" is a hand colored woodcut, size 11x17", edition 8. These Indian tipis were set a long time ago in the plains of South Dakota, but their spirit still linger there.

"New York, NY" is a hand colored woodcut, size 10x14", edition 8. Fire escape stairways on the back of buildings in New York City, USA are also a typical scene of the American cityscape.

Emily A. Reed

A Perfect End to the Day

Autumn Glory

"A Perfect End to the Day," - The painting was the # 1 image in "All Galleries" on ArtWanted.com on August 5, 2005. It was the winner of the "Endings and Beginnings" member challenge on that day.

"Autumn Glory" is an ArtWanted.com "Top Ten" rated photograph of burning bushes and other green and orange leaves taken behind the New Castle, Delaware public library in October, 2005.

Peace Orchids

"Peace Orchids" is a digital design based on a photo of orchids taken at Longwood Gardens, Kennett Square, PA, USA, and is a "Top Ten" rated design on ArtWanted.com.

Erika Brodie

The Break-Up

The Healing Process

The Break-Up: Watercolor; This peace is all about the expression and emotion of "the break-up". You see no color and the anger takes a place you didn't know existed. The bleeding rose was a touch of something that once was. www.artwanted.com/erikalynn

The Healing Process: Painted glass/Stained glass; This is about one of those days where you just feel you need a helping hand. You feel like you are drowning and God is there to shed the tears for you and share in hope. He lends you His healing power of strength. www.artwanted.com/erikalynn

Time-less Beauty

Time-less Beauty: Faux Painting on canvas; This is a young lady at heart so live and full of life. Innocent and sweet, but if you get up close she is aging and wrinkling. I think we see old people as "old" and hard of hearing and people who just don't do much. If you look closer, you see what's within', who they use to be, and they are beautiful just the way they are. We just need to take off the layers. www.artwanted.com/erikalynn

Greg Edwards

Star Light Curves

The Garden of Three Suns

The Garden of Three Suns (Iconography) A remote vision gift for Rapture Teachers where only wonder reaches...of a global garden in tri-color suns, where our Northern Lights help us encompas the beauty of neon life and the harmony we hold when walking on gold...and none to grow old, nor president!!! The only rule in loving this garden is the law of zero-population growth. 99.9% heaven. No animals to kill, we love all and get the proteins from synthesized grains that cover canine talons lost in another time and climb. Have faith my dear friends...

Star Light Curves: Star light curves, no straight line myths...in the key of catazone. Above time in geometric grooves, moveing to and fro freely in remote electric sown zone homes.

The Lost Sunset

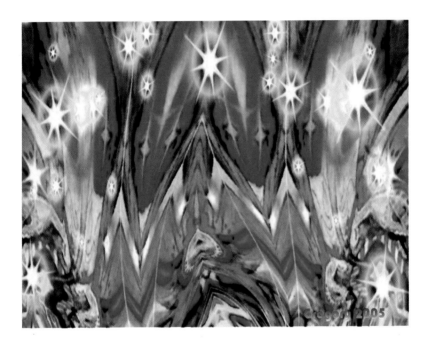

The Lost Sunset: We are all hanging on loosly, we are all in a higher love...How could we let go! ...then I realized the sunset trips. One a planet with three suns where there is no night. A red sun, a blue sun, and a yellow sun...says my long lost wife! There is no president nor heiarchy...just muse mode> ALL the time!!! Beautiful waters on cracked shells for sands, like emeral crystals. and birds swooning like feathered jely fish...[from my tape collection of five as my wife gave remote belief. She is gone to her next lesson.

Greg VandeVisser

Travels

Travels ©2002 Greg VandeVisser, A found object assemblage on wood.

Jan Kolling

From the Newborn Land

Taken from the series "Dostojefski Syndrome"

From the Newborn Land

Taken from the series "Dostojefski Syndrome"

Janet K. Brennan

Friends of Montecchia

"Oh no," I sobbed. Will I ever survive living in this strange and far away country?" Everything about it was foreign, and all I could think of was, "I want to go home!"

We had lost a daughter the year before to asthma, and the family was still in the midst of grieving, when military orders

Pagnotta di Roma

arrived for my husband, Arthur. They were sending us to the Veneto area, outside of Verona, Italy. I had lived in foreign countries before, yet this was very different. This tour of duty included no military housing, or friends nearby with which to communicate. Indeed, we were the only Americans within a fifty-mile radius, and no one in the tiny village of Montecchia di Crosara could speak English.

My children, Katie and Nicholas, took the train from the nearby village of San Bonafacio to school each day. Nicholas went west to his school in Verona, and Katie caught the eastbound train to the city of Vicenza, where her high school was located. Art's job took him fifty miles into the mountains. This he drove, in a tiny fiat. The fog was sometimes as thick as Pea Soup! Meanwhile, I stayed home in our villa for long hours each day. Often my family did not return until eight o'clock at night. We felt isolated in every sense of the word. Looking at this new assignment as a great learning experience seemed like an insurmountable task. Because of the stress of attempting to heal and return as an intact family after tragedy, we were most definitely, a family in crises. A hardship assignment to medieval Italy was the last thing in the world we wanted.

Many might say they would have envied out situation. Montecchia is an ancient village in the Soave province, nestled in the Valle di Alpone. It is surrounded by glorious vineyards, which produce both the red and green grapes that are used to make the delectable Soave wines. From the beginning of recorded history, this area was used for just such a purpose. In the distance, snow capped Alps ringed this Veneto area, and indeed the village itself enjoyed a mountain topped by a huge, wooden cross which seemed to stand guard over Montecchia.

We would need to adjust. We knew this. We would need to learn the language, and mingle as much as possible with our neighbors. This proved difficult as our Italian neighbors were as much intimated by us, as we were by them.

We had only been in our villa a few days when our Landlord, Signor Marcello Manubosco arrived at our door with his family. Introductions were made, and before long, we came to feel very much at home with the Manubosco family. They brought huge bundles of firewood for the cold winter, which lay ahead of us, and aptly demonstrated the art of baking Pizza over an open hearth. They invited us to their home to enjoy their fine hospitality, while sipping delicious wine which they produced themselves from their own vineyards.

In the spring, the Signore and his son, Giuseppe, plowed the area beside our home to make way for a garden. Both my husband and son new nothing about working the land; However, Giuseppe was kind enough to get them started. He showed them which vegetables did well in the rich, Italian soil that had already been farmed for centuries. Before long, vegetables were sprouting up from the ground, and as our village neighbors passed by on their evening strolls, they would stop to inspect the American Garden "Bravo . . . Bravo," they would shout. My husband and son were more than just a little proud. Working in the garden turned out to be very therapeutic. They spent long hours talking and working.

"A garden is more than just putting seeds into the ground," Signor Manubosco would tell us." It also produces food for the soul."

How right he was! We soon came to understand why every family in the village spent long, hours with their hands buried in the dirt of their own gardens.

Giuseppe often brought friends and relatives to our home, and our

View of Montecchia di Crosara, Italy

children soon began to meet the Italian children of the village. Children came. They were interested in learning how Americans played. Before long, friendships were established. Nicholas taught them the fine points of baseball, while they taught him the game of soccer. Katie spent afternoons on the

Villainmontecchia

front piazza, giggling with the Italian girls, and exchanging fashion ideas.

In the fall, the harvest of the grapes began. The Manubosco family invited us to join their entire family, cousins and all, to partake in picking the luscious fruit from the tender vines. They taught us to drink the natural juice from the grapes as we picked them so that we would not become thirsty. They also demonstrated the importance of singing while working. One could not work without at least one, good tenor amongst them. Often, if we were away for the day running errands, we would come home to find a huge basket of luscious grapes sitting in our foyer. It was wonderful to know that even though we were not out with them working in the vineyards, they were thinking of us.

It did not take long before we forgot that we were a family in mourning. We were, in fact, learning how to live again. We had become so busy with the challenge, our hearts, indeed our souls, forgot to cry. What we thought would be an impossible and sad experience suddenly became joyful, as we watched these beautiful villagers farm their land and harvest their grapes. We learned to dance with them at their festivals, and sing with them in their fields.

Needless to say, we will never forget the kindness of our wonderful Italian friends We are a lucky family, who learned the true meaning of friendship and love, and how easily it can transcend any cultural barriers.

We lived in Montecchia di Crosara for two years, all the while learning and growing as a family in a wonderful cultural exchange with our Italian neighbors. When we left that beautiful and ancient village, we felt secure in the knowledge that what we were taking with us, as well as what we were leaving behind, were memories of the richest sort. Oh, yes. Nick also left his baseball glove, Katie her teen magazines, Art his Fiat, and I, of course . . . left my heart.

Jean Ann Fitzhugh

Blackpool with its Famous Tower

Famous Cottage in North Wales Tu Hunt T'R Bont

JEM Wellen

Badalona in Catalonia Spain

TRY - OUT

experiment
trial and error
while you have somewhere to go
while your feet are walking

I have to go
still, here I sit
waiting for my train
I've been thinking all my thoughts
and feeling all my feelings

Left at an in between station
packed luggage at my feet
I've put my thoughts on stand-by
and my feelings on hold

only a gleaming point of light
at the back of my eyes
still tells of my longing
untill the train comes

The picture is from Badalona in Catalonia Spain. It is not a very romantic beach picture. But I used to live there and the rail road tracks just in front of the sea used to be a familiar site and sight. And a lot of beaches in the world are like that. Not exotic, just a place where people live.

The poem is about waiting at a station. But it could be waiting for all important results in life when we just took a risk to do something or go somewhere but sit there waiting to see what will come out of our decision.

Jennifer Johnson

Beached

Decembers Glory

Beached - The remains of this wrecked ship on the southern end of Hatteras Island are typically not visible, except after specific storms. Even the small waves take their toll each time the wreck is uncovered by the wind and tide. Black & white photo. Taken December 2004.

Decembers Glory - This breathtaking sunrise in December 2005, with the sunlight reflecting in the tidepools as the tide ebbed out, made me stop for a few minutes more than usual and remember just how blessed all of us, who get to live on Hatteras Island or just occasionally visit this piece of paradise, are to see our Creator's glory first-hand.

Foggy Bottom

About Hatteras Island:

Hatteras Island is one of a series of barrier islands off the coast of North Carolina which make up the Outer Banks. The island is more than 80 per cent National Park land, with seven small fishing villages scattered among the remaining area. The island is approximately 70 miles long and ranges from about 100 yards to a few miles wide. It boasts beautiful scenery and abundant wildlife, especially birds. It is the closest point to the Gulf Stream on the east coast of the United States, north of Florida. This creates some unusual and dramatic weather patterns, which in turn provide breathtaking sunrises and sunsets. The coast of Hatteras Island has been nicknamed, among other things, the "Graveyard of the Atlantic" because of the large number of shipwrecks on our treacherous shoals throughout history. This is an island rich in history, tradition and heritage, and a favorite spot for vacationers. Our lighthouse (the tallest brick lighthouse on the east coast) is recognized world-wide.

Foggy Bottom - A view of the dock on the Pamlico Sound behind our house, on a foggy, lick-calm day. The crab pot creates an optical illusion...is it the reflection of a hidden crab pot, or a crab pot with no reflection?

Jeremy R Meier

Window of Light

Window of Light (Study 2) - A former architect's residence in greater Los Angeles, California. Sharp beams of sunlight penetrate through openings amongst the building's exterior, and this late afternoon shaft of light bounces brightly off of the copper metal near the kitchen.

Jim Corbett

Sunmi's Triumphant Refill

Yatap Brook in the Green

Sunmi's Triumphant Refill - Korean coffee shops are famous for free refills and Sunmi returns with hers.

Yatap Brook in the Green - It is mid-March and green is growing throughout the shallow Yatap Brook in Seongnam City, S.Korea.

Joseph Ganley

Jim at Lake Massabesic

Lake, Iced Over

Joseph Steven Valencia

Village Sisters

Karen Pike

New 0rleans

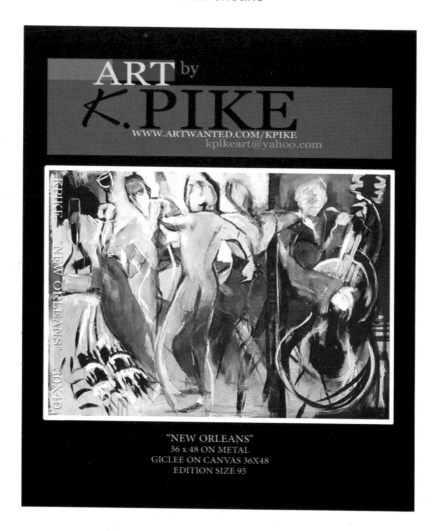

"NEW ORLEANS"
36 x 48 ON METAL
GICLEE ON CANVAS 36X48
EDITION SIZE 95

Parr

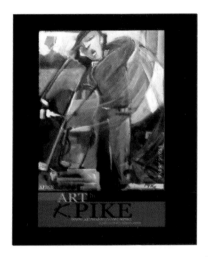

San Deigo Bay Poster

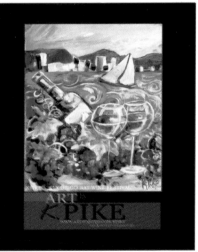

Kari Korhonen

Hunter

Hunter - Where we get our dreams is the place our minds go when the body dies.

Linnanneito2

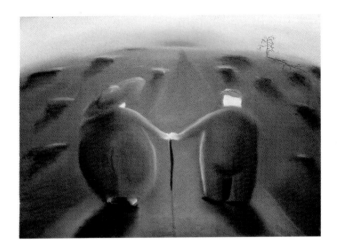

Perspective

Perspective - the arctic breeze.

Linnanneito2 - The gate before the eternity.

Kym Lovell

Daytripper

I have always believed the best way to learn is to travel. Try new things, be adventures, let loose, dream, explore and discover. I suppose you could say i was hungry for what i couldn't have. The canvas is divided into two sides, the right side being 'right now' school, work, assignments, Brisbane. This is provoked by the use of purple stamps down the canvas (late for school, late for class, homework not done). I cut into the canvas so i could stick little pieces of map behind it (Brisbane) to represent where I live/grew up. LONDON is in big bold letters , I traveled overseas when I was 11 and that has been a big part of me, a lot of family remain in England. Teabags are used not only to create interest but the brand of the teabags are bushells which is an Australian product.

On the left side of the canvas represent dreams, aspiration, places I wish to go. A paintbrush is stuck in the corner near a picture of the Eiffel Tower. Stitching is embedded/stitched into the canvas to represent eternity/memories are priceless and forever. Black pastel is roughly used to create the vibe of a map. In the middle of the canvas you can see a big browns smudge, this is actually a press of my naked body/face. Therefore i am in the middle of both sides. This is my mind right now, this is how messy and all over the place it is. Love is everything to me, love and travel and the journey of both.

MEDIA: acrylic paint, pastal, shalac, stamps, teabags, glue, envelopes, postage stamps, pictures, paintbrush, stitching...

L Lindall

3 Celestials

Vanilla Blues

"3 Celestials" is a pastel painting of three oriental teapots with some loose tea using soft pastels on Mi-Teintes acid free paper measuring 11 x 14.

"Vanilla Blues" is a pastel painting of two wine glasses with a wine decanter and vanilla beans using soft pastels on Mi-Teintes acid free paper measuring 11 x 14.

Lárus G

The Traveller

Linda Block

Blue Hill

Blue Hill, Empire, CO - This snow capped mountain sets a back drop, as strong and majestic Pines stretch to reach their full potential. This is a place to stop and feel the awesome forces of nature in balance.

Maroon Bells

Spring Gulch

The Maroon Bells, Aspen, Colorado - This is what calls people to Colorado and makes it even more difficult to leave. The spectacular Rocky Mountains . They give you a rush just to gaze at their awesomeness. The air is fresher and your step is lighter as you meander through endless pathways. May the peace of the wilderness be with you.

Spring Gulch, Carbondale, CO - It's late spring in the Rocky Mountains and the icy blue waters tumble forward. It's a refreshing respite from the bumpy and dusty road that brought you here.

Marguerite Carstairs

Baekje Military Museum at Baekje in South Korea

Surf Fishermen on the Beach at Surfers Paradise on the
Gold Coast of Queensland

The Great Wall at North Tower, Beijing China

Arches to Temple

The Acropolis Greece

The tour walked us right to the top of the Acropolis from which we could see all around and down to Athens, led by the academic who wrote the guide book, which would have been wonderful if I understood the language she used. However, the ruins were breathtakingly awesome and the camera worked overtime trying to capture all this splendour.

The Acropolis is right on the top of the mountain and viewed from all over Athens.

The Acropolis Hill was considered a sacred site, and is the most important site of the city.

As you climb the path to the top, the views are just breathtaking. Many of the ruins were under reconstruction and being renovated for the Olympic Games, during the time I climbed this monument.

During the classical period, three important temples were erected on this site and today you can still see the ruins of the temples. The Parthenon is still here, and can be viewed in its entirety...and many of the great arches and walls of the temple and the buildings that were here are still standing. The colors are fantastic.

You can view more of these ruins on my Travel site and also on my albums at Webshots.

Greece to me was the total photographer's delight with an image in every few steps. There was so much to see and photograph and experience in Athens and the islands.

I also loved the people, and the food and the bread and wine.

I love Greece.

Marie Calow

Looking for You

Journeys I find are always to ones self in the end. Where ever the search for good art takes me I always end up crossing water, watching water and skies and the way that humans interact under and around them. I often smile when I hear about the sophistication that 21st century affords us, you dont have to look far around any corner to see what we havn't achieved. We dont need to look further than the actual in nature to see where real dynamism is present, I'm always drawn to planet parts of the planet. The physics of light and chemistry of water and weather are sources of facination to me. I also zoom intlectually from the cosmology of nature right down to the detail in some of my works creating another minute landscape with in the macro one this world has no pleasing reference points and you must therefore negotiate your own.

Still Blue

Watch

I like having the wind in my face and capturing a part of something that will endure beyond myself. Some of the water work that I do is a seconds brilliant expression before being completely engulfed in water, water always prevails and I have almost lost a camera on more than one occasion. When I saw news shots of the tsunami last year I was unable to look at some of my work for a while and realised that the reference point for much of it had changed. I no longer feel quite so devastated in this way and recognise that if my rationale as discribed above is true then then I have to keep making work.

Michael Estabrook

Turks and Caicos Islands

Turks and Caicos

There's a coconut tree,
several of them, right outside our room,
clusters of large green orbs hanging
in the breezeless morning,
I can hear the ocean whispering
like hyperactive ghosts
in the background beyond the pool
and cabana bar, light-blue wavelets
slapping, gurgling in to shore,
beckoning, beckoning
for us to come on down and bake
the infernal civilization
out of our weary bones in the heat
of the ever-simmering sun.
No traffic or banks,
no bills or broken cars,
no ringing phones or leaves to rake,
only the pure clean sand and languid ocean,
and the ever-simmering sun
in Turks and Caicos grand, magnificent
island 90 miles off Hispaniola
and I had never even heard of them ever
until our son's best friend
invited us to his destination wedding there.

Turks and Caicos Resort

Mike Howe

Blue Bell Wood

Blue Bell Wood

My work is based on a blue bell wood which is near to sheffield south yorkshire UK, here its very peacefull & quite there are several woods in the area, much to explore, I have lived in sheffield all of my life upto now.

Mirsad Mehulic

In Clear Sea

In clear sea, watercolor on 140 Arches, size 14x21 in Fishing boat in clear Adriatic Sea

In Low Tide

Vis Port

In low tide, watercolor on 140lb Arches, size 17x21 in. Small fishing boats in safe harbor, island Vis - Adriatic Sea, Croatia.

Vis port, watercolor on 140lb Arches, size 18x21 in. Old houses and boats in part of town Vis port (Vis (Issa) Croatia)

Patricia Fritsche

If the Ships would Speak!

What would they say?
Of your monster ability to hold in your deep, mystifying, palm
the dreams of sailors disturbed at any time,
from a belly ache of yours. A sea monster persay,
causing much indigestion or a nagging cough,

rocking and swaying through the night
making your disposition to seaman a fearful lot.
Very jittery slapping away at the boldest wind
to challenge your strength to explore new lands.

But, also, would they attest to your natural charm?
Sun glistening just right, on your bodice, the internal rhythm displayed
a cool galantine your waters mimic.
When called to your peacefulness, pearly sails of strong lines and
heavy experienced wood are comforted so nicely, as you breathe out,
and carry on.

And dreams move forward, and our catalogued in someone's contemplation log,
as the travel beckons us on, and the vehicles to arrive
are chosen again. The sea grows anxious of any new encounters
the affair it may have again, to live with new and reborn sensations.

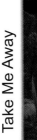

Take Me Away

The bonding of nature's elements captured in a landscape scene.

Patricia Wellingham-Jones

At the Outer Reaches of the Ranch

In a star-thistle field wind sweeps
across wild grasses stiff in winter
brown, iced tips. Foothills brood
dark in cloud-scudded sky, one quail
sounds its lonely cry.

I balance on earth's skin.

Feel lichen crusted on granite
beneath the sole of my shoe.
Hear the slow breath of snakes
asleep underground, waiting to stir
in the first warm gusts of spring.

Where the creek rolls stones like children's
marbles, I halt under a live oak, hair
caught in a low-hanging branch.
Dangle, doll-like,
among wind and time and deep-roaring fire.

California Ranch

Woodcarvers of Bali

Bali

Equatorial air hangs dense
with sawdust and sandalwood,
the flash of parrot feathers,
sound of rain dripping.

Young men and master sit cross-legged
on a thatched pavilion, calloused soles
tucked under batik sarongs, fingers deft
as fireflies darting magic.

Woodcarvers flash smiles
over thoughts hidden deep.
Slim brown hands wield rough tools,
gouge, rub, polish chunks whittled small.

Apply hacksaw, thin blade to forms
teased from fragrant wood
art developed for a god,
honed for the tourist trade.

The River Li: China, 1987

1.
On the current we glide
past water buffaloes
drowsy in midday sun.

Women under straw cones
bend low, add their sweat
to rice they tend in paddies.

2.
Hollow ring the karst hills
in crystal echoes.

From high ledges bells dangle,
jangle, whisper, invite.

Bats swoop, dark wings pulsing
among limestone pillars.

Junk on River Li, China

Deep inside lanterns shimmer,
clear drops slide in the silence.

3.
Upstream on the dock a man
with fishing birds yoked to his shoulders
glares at tourists aiming cameras, ignoring
his outstretched hand.

Shrill voices in the market
clamor for passing coins
over the insistent wash
of the river.

Pepita Selles

A Swedish Girl in Spain Looking at a Gigant Peacock

Collage from Parts of the World. Sheels from the Maldives and Swedish Fauna

Our Swedish Wood Santas in Swedish Winter Landscape

Phil Kunin

Empire State Bldg

NY Street

Reflection of New York

Rebecca L Phillips

Golden Bough ... Autumn Night

Spirit Guide to the Third Eye

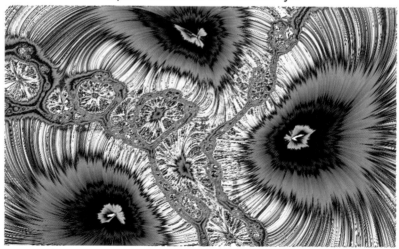

Golden Bough ... Autumn Night - A vision, as my eyes opened from my nightime sleep. A bough of autumn leaves in golden hue, lit with moonlight the leaves flowing, falling so gently with intensely delicate grace. One of my life's best nights...repleat with a dream, made in reality.

Spirit Guide to the Third Eye - She is the spirit guide of the third eye, friendly and loving she wears a tattoo of sorts on her forehead...a sign of her mission to Humankind. On the day I spoke with her for this picture, she was looking a bit like a Panda (oh, how she loves all lifeforms, all creation). Just allow yourself to be in her presence, and you will Learn!

Volcanic Beachead

Volcanic Beachead - The volcanic epoch of Earth had quelled. The skies having begun to clear, and the waters having started to cool, the Great Mother is already mapping-out the plan for life on Earth.

Robert L. Bills

Bird Island

Great Egrets

These shots include a Connecticut warbler in Daytona Beach. Note the Bee on the flowers. The other two shots are of a Snowy Egret in breeding plumage. They were taken with a Canon D20 digital camera with 8.2 megapixels.

Robin M Buehler

Cypress

Cypress was also taken in Florida. I was driving around, sightseeing in the vicinity where my uncle was living at the time and came across this exotic, fairyland-ish scene I knew I needed to photograph. It reminded me of something that should be in a fairy tale.

Emerald Memories

Look Out Point

Emerald Memories was taken at a theme park near Orlando, Florida and it reminded me of a trip I took back in 2002 to Ireland. It was my first trip outside the USA, other than Canada and Bermuda years ago. One of my ancestors on my maternal grandmother's side is from County Down, North Ireland. So, this trip "home," even if it was the republic (of Ireland) it felt good.

Look Out Point was taken in Asheville, North Carolina, on the grounds of the Biltmore Estate. The estate is one of my favorite places to be, especially over the Christmas holidays, when the place is decorated. This particular spot overlooks some of the gardens. In summer, it must be a spectacular view!

Roger Cummiskey

Under Construction

Gibraltar Remembered

Gibraltar Remembered 35 x 24 cms, watercolour - There are quite a number of references to Spain and the Andalusian women in Molly Bloom's soliloquy at the end, last 30 pages, of Ulysses, by James Joyce. In this sequence Molly is reminiscing on her experiences of seeing the flair and the excitement of Flamenco dancing while she lived with her father in Gibraltar. This whole passage in Ulysses uses the "stream of consciousness" technique, which Joyce brought to literature for the first time. The section is referred to as Molly Bloom's soliloquy or the Penelope episode/chapter. ©2006.

Under Construction 40 x 20 cms, watercolour - I wrote this poem to honour James Joyce and decided to turn it into a painting but as the poem is about two pages long I just used some of it. When Joyce was writing Finnegans Wake over 15 years he always referred to it as Work-in-Progress when asked what the title would eventually be. I use the modern day equivalent as the present title until such time as I get around to finishing the poem. I began writing the poem in 1998 and have had three Construction updates since. Maybe you would like to give it a title? ©2006.

Joyce -- the Pluralist (Paris)

Joyce -- the Pluralist (Paris) 46 x 61 cms, watercolour - This is a watercolour painting, in the style popularized by Andy Warhol, taken from a photograph of James Joyce (1882-1941) in Paris in 1920 at the door of the famous bookshop, Shakespeare and Co. owned by Joyce's friend, the American, Sylvia Beach. She was a patron and the first publisher of "Ulysses". At this time, while constantly short of funds, Joyce had started to dress in a dandified fashion. This original painting is based on that photograph. ©2005.

Sandra Busby

Florence in the Rain

Paris Bridge at Night

San Marco Cafe

Capturing light and reflection as they mingle and fuse, her images have an "other-worldly" quality. Busby's use of mirrors and windows creates an inverted image which gives the viewer imaginary access.

Shari Travison

"Laguna Beach at Dusk" (Laguna Beach, CA)

"Laguna Beach at Dusk" (Laguna Beach, CA) - Laguna Beach, California is located along the Pacific Ocean in the County of Orange. It has approximately seven miles of beautiful scenic coastline consisting of bluffs, homes, coves, tide pools & beaches. The city of Laguna Beach is also known for its boutiques, numerous Art Galleries, Festivals, Spas, and Resorts. In the summer, you can visit one of its Festivals including the Festival of Arts, Sawdust Festival, and Pageant of the Masters. Laguna Beach has many enjoyable tourist attractions and is considered a Resort town.

Shirley Bolstok

Peru, the Ancient One
(Tienes Ojos Bellos)

Her ancient soul steals upon the landscapes
Her footsteps rippling through the coastal seas
The Valleys and Hillsides are her dress as it drapes
over the Llamas creating a soft and gentle breeze
Her Dark Incan eyes move in ways of mystery
It is only she who remembers, only she knows
She holds her head proud and bears her secrecy
Peru, oh beautiful land , tienes ojos bellos
You have seen the death of your Incan children
The cities are now empty that were filled with gold
You bear the grief of the forgotten knowledge of then
The ancient ways have departed with wisdom untold
The stones have fallen away upon the mountain side
where the footsteps once walked upon Machu Piccu
The tall peaks carry voices of the civilization that died
We cannot understand the dream that you knew
Beautiful Peru, tienes ojos muy bonitos
You have kept your dress green and the skies blue
When you walk among the land your splendor grows
The violet waters of the land reflect the sun
You are the ancient one, you were here before
When the earth moved, you were the one
You are the exquisite woman of the old folklore
Yours are the eyes of the dark side of the sun

Machu Piccu Peaks

Machu Piccu

Machu Piccu

Machu Piccu

I was in Peru in July, 2003

Song of the Tetons

Oh beautiful song of winds gone by
Towering peaks rise into Violet skies
Secrets revealed through legends told
Mystery remains in wisdom of old
A green cloak woven of hills in Spring
My soul beckons to the melody you sing
Magnificent Tetons, so still and so grand
You've stolen my heart upon the bow of your land
Essence eternal merged and entwined
Perfection tremendous, radiant and divine
Amethyst temples are roses in bloom
With arid scent of sweet perfume
In your strength, I feel vulnerability of age
I see the universe in forests of sage
Forever engraved in tablets of time
Imparting your spirit from fields of pine
Oh, Grand Tetons, raised from heavenly sod
Your white peaked snowcaps,
the pure flowers of God

Tetons

I was in the Grand Tetons in Jacksonville, WY- United States and wrote this poem in honor of them in May of 2002.

Steven P. Love

Bridge to Nowhere

Imminent Domain

"Bridge to Nowhere" was taken during a business trip to the Arizona town of Superior. It's an old bridge that seems to parallel Highway 60 but it was abandoned when Arizona built a new bridge over Queen Creek and by-passed it. If you look close you can see vegetation growing on the bridge. This photo is for sale as a 13 inch by 19 inch print for $35. You can get the details by visiting my site or email me at sales@deepdesertent.com

"Imminent Domain" was originally a film photo that I took 10 years ago. It shows an abandoned farm house that was later demolished to make way for a power plant near the Arizona town of Arlington. This photo is also free to anyone that wants a copy for themselves. But as you can see the quality is not as good as my newer photos because the original is on film and film degrades with time. If you wish to have a free copy of it you may email me at sales@deepdesertent.com

Smokey

The Face That Launched
A Thousand Words

"Smokey" is a photo I took from my own property where I was watching the smoke drifting into Arizona from the California wildfires that erupted in 2005. This photo is also for sale as a 13 inch by 19 inch print for $35. For details please visit my site or email me at sales@deepdesertent.com

"The Face that Launched a thousand Words" was just an accidental shot in which I caught my cat, named Moonlight, yawning. I found the picture so inspirational that I have also used it as a reference for two artworks that can be viewed at my website. This photo is free for anyone to use. If anyone is interested in a copy they can email me at sales@deepdesertent.com

Sam Stearman

Inle Lake - The Place That Time Forgot

Ever want to get away from it the hectic pace of everyday life; the bombardment of sights and sounds of urban life; and people people everywhere all rushing to get someplace else. Ever wish you could step back in time to a simpler life free from the stress and the problems associated with all the ills that have come with rogress I do -- and I found such a place.

The place is Inle Lake and it is in Myanmar (formerly Burma) in SE Asia. It is the perfect place to step back in time and enjoy the life much as it was a hundred or more years ago. Inle Lake is located 3,000 feet high up in the mountains of Shan State, reachable by an hour plane trip from either Yangon or Mandalay to neighboring Heho and another half-hour journey by car.

Inle Lake is, in a word, serene. The lake and the scenery are enchanting, hazy in the mornings, sunny with billowing clouds in the afternoon and alive with color at sunset.

Visiting Inle Lake is leaving the world, its hustle and bustle and its frantic pace, far far behind -- like stepping into another time and place -- indeed a paradise of peace, tranquility and harmony.

Lone boat on lake, late afternoon. While waiting on the lake for the sun to set, I took this picture looking east toward the opposite shore

The people of Inle Lake, some 70,000 of them, live in four cities bordering the

Night view from our lodge

Lone fisherman in the early morning mist.

Inle Lake famed leg-rowing fisherman with conical net. They catch fish by capturing fish inside the net and spearing them.

lake, in numerous small villages along the lake shores and on the lake itself. Most live in simple stilt houses of woven bamboo and are largely self-sufficient, living much as their forefathers did.

In addition to fish caught by their picturesque "leg-rowing" fishermen, they actually raise vegetables and fruits on gardens floated on the surface of the lake and carry on small industries with hand labor to produce goods for local use and trading. Their five-day markets, which rotate between different places around the lake, serve as the basic shopping alls with sales conducted from boats on the lake.

But it is the fact that neighbors help fellow neighbors in time of need that reminds me of more innocent days in the U.S., before drugs, before

Floating gardens are used to grow both fruits and vegetables on the lake itself

rampant crime and before fears of security. They are simple people, living simple lives, with boats as their only means of

11 year-old Padung girl. As girls get older, additional neck bands are added. Adults have 25.

Lively grandmother. You can see the story of her life in her face, and it has been good.

Two ladies, of different cultural backgrounds, living and working together in peaceful harmony.

transportation.   Long boats carry produce and tourists, some with motors, leaving rooster tails in their wake.   Residents cook and heat with wood.   Many residents still do not have electricity. Step back in time when you view these pictures -- then put Inle Lake on the top of your vacation list.   It is truly a place that is timeless.

Two native men looking manly for the camera

As a traveler/photographer, the most important considerations are to make sure you bring lots of film and keep your camera handy, because from sunrise to late night, it is a photographer paradise. All my shots were with my trusty Olympus C-2100, with its 10X zoom.   With such beauty, you don need special lenses and filters just let the lake and its people speak for themselves.

Just your typical sunset on Inle Lake   Young monk, two windows

Tabitha L. Borges

Ancient Times

Rape

"Ancient Times" Picture of Della Benvenuto Cellini's Perseus Beheading Medusa Taken at Piazza Della Signora in Florence, Italy taken with Canon Rebel XT Dec 2005

"Rape" picture of "The rape of the Sabine Woman" In Piazza Della Signora in Florence, Italy with Canon XT Dec 2005

Tatiana Pahlen

On the Streets of Stockholm

Truly, Sweden is a wonderland. Since 1901, this enchanting kingdom is the mother country of the Nobel Prize, seeking out the nominees from all over the globe. In the Blue Room of the City Hall, where those fortunate winners emerge to collect their prizes, you would not find a tiny trace of blue. Seating capacity is no more than 1,300 guests.

The construction of City Hall began in 1911.

I'm warning you, it's almost impossible to fall from the stairs leading to the banquet tables, even for a badly drunken nominee. The main architect, Ragnar Ostberg, while work was in progress, urged his wife Elsa to run up and

Eric and Tatiana on the stairs of the City Hall

down the stairs, dressed in her evening gown and high heels, to assure of everyone's safety. Immediately after they opened in 1923, Elsa ran down the stairs for the last time and for good. Without saying adieu, she left her architect.

My heart was pounding as I climbed these very stairs, that decades earlier, the great writer and poet Ivan Bunin, the first Russian Nobel Prize winner, mounted in 1933. Let me introduce you to the other Russian winners in Literature. In 1965, from the Don River spreading the smell of tractor fumes, the literal larcenist, Mikhail Sholokhov, entered the City Hall. During the Civil War, Sholokhov stole a manuscript from a dead soldier's pocket. He made four books out of it; this instantly became a classic of Soviet Literature. Then he produced thirty more, based on the same stolen goods. Unfortunately, Boris Pasternak was forced to decline his award in 1958. He created a striking and much loved by every soul outside of Russia masterpiece,"Doctor Zhivago." For that he was shunned to death by his comrade-writers who suspended his designated writer's membership then cut him off from a literary community.

In 1970, Alexander Solzhenitsyn rightfully earned the prize; he was earlier expelled from the Gulag before being axed and deported from the Soviet Union for his studious and breathtaking Archipelag Gulag. In 1987, the torch went to Joseph Brodsky, who was booted from the Soviet paradise soon after as well.

There was another candidate that declined his prize. A French novelist-philosopher, a self-proclaimed existentialist, Jean-Paul Sartre, a winner in 1964, nobly bowed out of his nomination in protest to the values of bourgeois society. Ironically, Mr. Sartre lived a bourgeois life himself, much like his mentor Karl Marx.

My abysmal thoughts faded as I overheard the tourists' voices, buzzing around me. I left the Blue Room hoping to be back one day. Birger Jarl built Stockholm in 1252. The City sits cozily on the water and attracts the attention of countless immigrants. The endless flow of tourists also helps overrun the City: most of them Japanese and Americans. They can be easily recognized by their worn sneakers, baseball hats and shorts, all disdained by well-heeled Europeans.

Swedish television widely broadcasts guidance on how to survive the locust-like invasion of foreigners. The simplest way is taking an excursion to one of the archipelagos by using the tourist's boat, where for some rather odd reason, the tourists' sneakers don't gather. They all jumble in the center of the old City, called Gamla Stan. Currently the archipelagoes are becoming the hiding places for the local VIPs.

The biggest crime is jumping ahead of the line, which builds in front of the tiny cafeterias, one sees all over the town. It looks like nobody works here; everybody spends their time gulping coffee or beer. Official working hours is from 7 to 4. After four, the idle line doubles at the restaurants. But 17% of the citizens that didn't join these lines are most likely on the suicide watch, which is a rapidly growing segment in Scandinavia. The highest rate, 28%, stays steadily in Finland. The lack of light in wintertime

Tatiana in The Blue Room at The City Hall, Stockholm in July, 2000

and the lack of excitement on the streets incite those hopeless folks to take their lives for the sake of the event itself. There is plenty of light in the summer: all night long . . . Really, when you don't need it. One must be totally drunk to tolerate the brilliant sunrays bursting through the double curtains and keeping you awake all night.

I've heard some legends about the good-hearted reigning Queen Silvia. Passing the palace guards, its Majesty often treats the young watchmen with Haagen Dazs and rarely scolds them for the dingy buttons on their blue uniforms.

These days the Swedish Government is plotting to pull three million tax dollars from the working class in order to multiply the frogs. The plan is to design three lakes for the three different types of frogs. That's because the cold-blooded families couldn't dwell together in the same pool. No Frenchman is allowed near these areas! The Government requirement is to keep the frogs' legs attached to their bodies.

Therefore the question was raised, how to feed these rascals? Their usual meal is the bloodthirsty mosquitoes and flies, which could not exist without regular donors. Many volunteers with superb blood records are relocating to the special zones to save the vanishing green skinned clan. Swedish researchers are well aware of the lesson with the dinosaur. They're taking this phenomenon of disappearing frogs to a superlative level. Some of them from a magic kiss of Scandinavian femme fatales, would turn into charming princes. Perhaps, this would end the overseas passages with all those Swedish vixens in search for the alien princes, because their local folks, as they're revealing, are icier than stillborn frogs.

Tatiana next to the mausoleum of Birger Jarl - the founder of Stockholm in 1252

They're all welcoming Russians: they love them there. Russian words are heard everywhere, mostly at the shoe stores. Shoes in Stockholm are cheap and durable like the lifestyle of this country. A twenty five percent tax is added on everything, including groceries. Water is pure and directly from the tap is tastier than Evian.

In the Summer the sun is scorching, but don't get fooled. Remember, never venture outside without a sweater. Despite the heat during the daytime hours, it's chilly after 5 p.m. But if you forgot to bring it along, don't worry, the trendy bars and restaurants will offer you a woolen quilt. You may notice these striped mountains of blankets on every chair.

After a week in Stockholm, I only counted six hobos: quiet, modest, and neatly dressed. No one hits you on the head with a brick, pushes you under the train or begs. People seem to mind their own business: the homeless are drifting around and picking the drained beer cans from the spotless garbage baskets.

The subways are cleaner than American hospitals. You won't view the art of graffiti, won't sniff urine down there. You don't see the signs: "Curb your dogs." There are no dogs on the streets. Needless to say, when you walk, you don't have to look down. The Swedes drive their canines to the park; they think it's brutal for their loved ones to touch the ground lacking grass.

You don't hear this word stress: it does not exist in their lexicon. And, of course, it doesn't slip from tongues of the visitors arriving to dip their fatiqued bones into this mirthful environment in the Summer.

Truly, Sweden is a wonderland!

Tazda Lawson

Phoenix Eggling

Red Draj

Red Witch

Trisha Allard

Crashing Waves

Sun Goes Down

Crashing Waves - The image was taken at Depot Bay, Newport Oregon. It is of the Rocks and Cliff in a lil alcove. It was a beautiful spring day at the ocean and the weather was unusaul. It was taken in the Spring of 2005.

Sun goes down - One of my favorites. It was taken along the coastal highway in Oregon. The sun was going down behind some clouds, and the golden colors were just amazing.

Sunset at NyeBeach

Sunset at NyeBeach - The image is a Sunset taken at NyeBeach, Newport, Oregon in the spring of 2005. I was taking a long walk on the beach as the sun went down. The colors were so awesome I couldn't resist Taking sever pictures.

Yvonne Sparkes

Impressions of India

Feb/March 2005

You love her, or hate her, adore her, abhor her.
You try to forget her, but you cannot ignore her.
She is full in your face when her masses are teeming,
With the beauty of rivers, when her looks are for dreaming.
A Peacock with a greeting, to meet early morning,
Or a sunrise on The Ganga, with a new day for dawning.
The home of The Tiger, The Pachyderm and Deer,
The Python, The Cobra, all the snakes that you fear.
An abundance of bird life with colours full measure,
The Banyan, and the Bodhi, lovely trees for your pleasure.
The Raj and the Moghul, the land of the caste,
She has joined the new century, but clings to the past.
A land of the Sari, the Rickshaw and such,
Where the Cow and the Pig bar the way for the clutch.
A chaotic rhythm of animals and man,
All over the road and a big traffic jam.
It`s a nightmare and hell, to survive there each day,
But, the smile of her people, interacts and will stay.
Their nature is friendly, and generous and kind,
The loveliest of people, that you`ll ever find.
Such a joy to remember and to keep in my heart,
This small part of my India will never depart.

Sunrise on the Ganga

Written with affection for the people of India

Alan Morgan

ARUNACHALA

And when you reach your Arunachala
Just as the sun touches the horizon.
When you find your holy hill
rose tinted by the glory of the clear, morning light.
Just stand.
In awe and wonder.
No need to say anything.
For you understand in a different way.
A way which cannot be confined in words.
So when that moment comes
hold out your hands.
The future flows towards you.
Stretch out your hands
ready for the seeds,
the seeds of time.

Alice Parris

THE MARKINGS OF CAIN

I hear the cries of Cain as he was
driven out of Paradise. I see the scorpion-like
mark upon his forehead forcing him to move from city to city.
His offering, like mine was paltry,

light-suffused, lacking a bloodier substance.
I have been driven out of one relationship after
another, being charged with heinous crimes-
by man but not by my Maker.

I labor in self-pity like Sisyphus,
lamenting the pushing of a boulder uphill.
I am told that I am not a star-child wandering.
"Arise, put on your armor. You are a soldier
of light in a lost and dying world. Arise."

I shake off remorse like beads of water upon
the feathered. I am renewed daily by drops
of dew. I begin to train again like a gladiator
who is destined to battle once again in the
Familiar arena of merciless decadent earth..

As a punishment from the gods, in the underworld, Sisyphus was compelled to roll a big
stone perpetually up a steep hill; but before it reached the top of the hill the stone always
rolled down, and Sisyphus had to travel up the hill all over again.

Floriana Hall

OHIO ROLLING ALONG

Wagons rolling, bumping, thumping along,
Pioneers' hardships masked by laughter and song,
Started out from states east to territories west,
Stopped to give Ohio's fertile soil a test.

Beautiful streams and scenery,
Deciduous trees and greenery,
Seasonal climate appealed to all,
Gardens in summer, harvest in fall.

Farmers prospered, cities grew to be,
States rights in March eighteen hundred three,
The first capital was Chilicothe,
And Thomas Worthington, it's father, you see.

Ross County built the first statehouse
And was the site of the first courthouse,
The bicentennial celebration starts there,
And bells will be cast at Akron's CityFaire.

Cuyahoga Valley National Park covers much land
A scenic railway ride from Peninsula to expand.
Indians and pilgrims crossed this ground
Along the Cuyahoga River, forests abound.

Columbus, our present capital, will rejoice
With a festival on the fourth of July,
Tall ships show on Lake Erie's North Shore,
A wagon train and flight celebration, much more.
Bicentennial Commission selected fifty-three
Historical markers by Ohio Historical Society
To help Ohioans learn about their state,
Song "Beautiful Ohio" to commenorate.

Our state which gave flight, eight presidents,
First person to walk on moon, Ohio resident,
This year the nation's top college football team,
We look with pride at these facts and beam.

TREASURE BY THE SHORE

Cleveland was never a mistake by the lake
Although other cities may have called it that —
From industry, ethnic, racial diversity
To the Jake,
To the Rock-N-Roll Hall of Fame
Where the Beatles, Elvis, & Kiss are famous names,
To the Great Lakes Science Center
With its weather forecaster and rocket flight simulator,
It's bubble machine, shadow and tornado maker,
A hot air balloon that rises to the top,
To Playhouse Square, Euclid Avenue, Tower City to shop,
To the Flats, Quicken Arena, the Cavs,
The return of the Browns football team,
Cleveland, Ohio, is Lake Erie's spectacular scene.

Jan Oscar Hansen

TROY

The military helicopter, as a last gesture, took me to
the village North Spain of I had left years ago to fight
in the world's many wars; limping, wars had taken its
toll; in to the square I only saw young faces, a new
generation, too late I had no business being here where
I only remembered the bygone and a dog I loved.

Opened cobwebbed doors and shuttered windows sun,
so long denied the room flooded in; later when night
fell I heard a scratch on my front door and there was
Troy, my dog I thought had died long ago, old now
wagging a grey tail. "So my boy what now, we are both
ancient and who's going to look after us now?"

TRUCKDRIVER

It was raining the morning when the eldest lady
in the village died, a tunnel of light came down
from the sky and inside it her soul flew up, plus
and outline of her face (for archive purposes,)
the relatives were left crying over a human husk.

A truck driver died but was brought back to life
thanks to the old lady's soul that just happened
to be nearby; the female soul now drives a ten
ton truck, the driver's mates are amazed he used
to drink plenty of ale, now he only drinks tea.

TRAVEL TO THE MOON

The plane that got lost ended up on the wrong side
of the moon where pale bananas are the only food,
the passengers made the pilot king because he had
four golden rings on his uniform, the co pilot a prince
and the stewardesses, princesses. There is not much
variety with bananas you can cook them, fry or eat
them raw and after a few month people revolted, was
it not so that it was the pilot who had miss navigated
and got them into this mess, he and his uniformed
flunkies slept inside the plane while they had to sleep
under it. They revolted and the House of Pilot was
pushed off the moon. Leaderless now and with the seed
of sedition sown their hearts they descended into chaos
and killed each other when the pale banana crop failed;
the one who survived took abode in the plane where he
starved to death amongst miniature bottles of booze.

This poem is about oil

Jerry Bradley

MAP

if I drew the place I knew
and not those distant places
I thought I knew

my heart could touch the map
where you are

and say to itself
without leaving home

if you are not there
you are here

ONE FOR THE ROAD

When the copter left and we were alone,
glacial ice splitting under our feet
and rinsing, rushing into the cavern's green glaze,
I thought of margaritas, the beach,
Puerto Vallarta's endless surf.
In moonboots and slicker I expected
a distant constellation, a landscape
pocked and lunar, ravaged, not the slush
of tequila in an icy lagoon.
But home
is so strange; tired of it, we leave
only to find ourselves reflected in chips
and cubes at every destination
and in return bringing part of what
was already us back to itself.
So when the pilot reappeared, lowering
with a friendly wave, we boarded
blooming with excitement and tipsy
from the cold while the swizzle of the rotor
lifted us once more and stirred our memory
like a strong drink.

SUNDAY DRIVE

traveling over a land teeming with color
we follow the map's direction

toward backroads and bayous
and into the flowering confection

of thickets that lure us with thorns
every sidetrack heavy with the promise

of something we should not miss
and every flower and tree

named, every last one
sweeter than a calorie on our tongues

as we push further still
into our dessert

reading the guide, alert
for the waterfall, the mill

the scenic overlook
beyond the ridge

Michael Estabrook

PARALLEL UNIVERSE

This vacation resort with its coconut palm trees
swaying in the warm tropical
island breezes, while majestic white herons fly
like albino horses, like Pegasus,
from tree top to tree top,
and gecko lizards leap like tiny green monkeys
across paths in and out of mangrove green shrubbery;
this island with its warm waves and sand,
sailboats, catamarans, giant sea turtles
and conch shells, pink as babies ears,
is simply a mirage, I know it,
a Caribbean mirage. Too bad I couldn't
take this mirage with me tomorrow morning
when I fly 6 and a half hours back
to civilization with its incessant traffic
and online banking, doctors appointments
and the room that needs wallpapering,
with its 8-to-5 grind and autumn leaves
filling the yard. Seems I'm
in the wrong parallel
of a parallel universe and can't get out.

EVERY DAMN MINUTE OF IT

Three beautiful young women
before me in the ocean,
shimmering islands in the blue-green,
two blondes and one
with lustrous brown hair, the bride-to-be.
And I'm thinking (of all things)
of the three goddesses at the wedding
of Thetis and King Peleus of Greece
way back in prehistory,
Paris giving the golden apple of discord
to Aphrodite (the brown-haired beauty)
confirming her as the most beautiful,
incurring thereby the eternal wrath
of Athena and Hera, the spurned goddesses,
all expecting of course
to be proclaimed as the most beautiful
of all the goddesses.
But, he got Helen in the bargain
and I know that after it all
was said and done, after ten long years
of war and bloodshed and destruction,
Paris would say without any hesitation
that the wrath and war,
the bloodshed and destruction
was worth it, worth
every damn minute of it.

Patricia Fritsche

IF THE SHIPS WOULD SPEAK!

What would they say?
Of your monster ability to hold in your deep, mystifying, palm
the dreams of sailors disturbed at any time,
from a belly ache of yours. A sea monster persay,
causing much indigestion or a nagging cough,

rocking and swaying through the night
making your disposition to seaman a fearful lot.
Very jittery slapping away at the boldest wind
to challenge your strength to explore new lands.

But, also, would they attest to your natural charm?
Sun glistening just right, on your bodice, the internal rhythm
displayed
a cool galantine your waters mimic.
When called to your peacefulness, pearly sails of strong lines and
heavy experienced wood are comforted so nicely, as you breathe out,
and carry on.

And dreams move forward,
and our catalogued in someone's contemplation log,
as the travel beckons us on, and the vehicles to arrive
are chosen again. The sea grows anxious of any new encounters
the affair it may have again, to live with new and reborn sensations.

where a disused barn,
idle cows and a covered bridge

herald the stopping point
and our unnamed X

a tree bulging with the prospect
of our picnicking in its shade

and a nap of chocolate and outdoor sex
there within close reach

where afterward like sufficient cows
we drowse into waves

and elaborate the lazy lake
like petals dreaming a peach

Robert Wilson

MY HAWAII

I've never visited Hawaii, except for a short stop as a child
on a troopship with civilian survivors liberated by U.S. Marines
from a Japanese prisoner-of-war camp in Shanghai.

The travel documentaries usually show surfers and Hawaiian
dancers. My surfing was done growing up on California beaches,
sometimes snorkeling off Palos Verdes

through long, submerged grasses and schools of fluttering fish.
A swimming partner and I once tracked a young leopard shark
along the sandy bottom until he speared it.

These memories fill my backyard now, with its view of the roiling
Rio Grande flanked by Bosque and Cottonwoods and distant
Spanish-broom-framed Sandia peaks.

Hawaiian plumeria doesn't flower in New Mexico but my grove
of forest bamboo hugging an Oriental bridge across a dry-bed
stream is scented by honeysuckle and trumpet vines.

I'll skip the crowded airports and airline trips, and paying high
prices to sleep in hotel beds previously slept in by thousands
of others doing God knows what.

Or the herds of stressed tourists as they stampede to the next
trap like grunions flopping on the beach. If I went, I would want
to know the natives. Maybe I'd even learn to Hula.

Until then, the backyard is my Hawaii.

BON APPÉTIT

In Paris last summer, a young man came to my door.

I asked qu'est-ce que vous voulez, monsieur?

He mumbled something, leading me to believe he was a tourist.

It was very hard to understand him because he was gnawing his hand.

I assumed he was nervous but maybe it was just hunger.

I asked him again, in English, what he wanted. Again, mumbling.

It's not nice to speak with your mouth full.

Only now he was also drooling on his hand.

I offered him a bottle of ketchup but he pushed it away.

Then I got an idea. Maybe he wanted dessert.

All I had was ice cream. But that didn't work either.

By now his hand was becoming very red and raw.

I was glad his other hand was still fresh.

It might come in handy on a long trip.

Finally, I figured out he wanted directions

to the nearest Burger King.

Wishing him bon appétit, I sent him on his way.

THE ICEBERG WHO SMILED AT ME

On a recent transatlantic flight
I glanced through the window
at a family of icebergs below.
In front was Big Daddy and Mama,
with two towering white peaks,
obviously not ashamed of nudity,
floating on a southward course.
What caught my eye was one
of their many children smiling up
at me. It was not a trick of sunlight.
A clearly distinguishable smile flashed
in my direction from a cute, young
female iceberg. I knew she was
female for the same reason I knew
who Mama was. This young lady
was not only smiling, but flirting.
No snow queen, she was anything
but glacial. Fortunately, nearby
passengers were all napping as,
unnoticed, I tearfully poured
my most intimate desires on the
maiden beneath me. Our tryst,
however, did not last long due to
the swiftness of the airplane
and I was soon sighing adieu as
she and her family drifted into
tropical waters and inevitable
but blissful dissolution somewhere
off the coast of Africa.

Robin M Buehler

IRELAND

A land so lush and green
Like nothing I've ever seen
On either side of this gray-blue pond.
Our people were, for centuries, torn asunder.
In the name of religion, it was all a blunder
That, to this day, dampened our nation's bond.
Thousands spoke of peace; for years it had not come
Until the day all of Ireland could call the emerald isle home.

MEMORIES OF HOME

Memories of home
of a distant emerald shore
from America

Yvonne Sparkes

LAKELAND`S WINTER

She`s had icing sugar sprinkled on her brow
She was glorious then, but oh just see her now.
Contours of white adorns each ridge and peak.
A cloud covers all, and the sun plays hide and seek.

Each plant and tree wears a gown of white.
Soft billows thrown, falling in the night.
A stretch of beauty amidst a landscape rare,
With frozen petals framing Lakeland`s hair.

Cascading waterfalls have for the moment ceased.
Those frozen rivulets enfold each seam and crease.
A prism of colour shines for my delight,
Greeting rays of bright new morning`s light.

The mountain tops bathed in snowy clouds,
Covered by an angry winter`s shroud,
And breath now steams from animals and man
To greet the birth of winter`s little lamb.

Now amidst the cold and bitter nip,
Of winter`s wind, blown with a fiercesome whip.
This joy of such a rich and lovely scene
Still takes my heart, as well as all the green.

Written in appreciation of the beauty of our English Lake District where I have been
a frequent visitor over the years.

Andrew McIntyre

THE BIG MAN

I read the telegram. Marshall dead. Proceed Port Campbell immediately. So Marshall was dead. One of our best men. I lit a cigarette, wondering how he might have died. There had been an outbreak of cholera recently. I knew he hadn't been well. Poor old Marshall. I remembered a large fellow, clipped mustache, very English. My wife brought whisky. I have to go to Port Campbell, I said, Marshall's dead, I've got to close the negotiations. She paused for a few seconds, Oh dear, how awful. How long will it take? I don't know, I replied, A couple of days perhaps. I stared into the dark, the oil lamp flickering in the slight breeze.

Marshall had been very close to concluding the business. A matter of formalities. The consortium was about to control a quarter of the region's gold. We were going to mine an area bigger than London. Negotiations to resolve, apparently some of the natives' demands were still creating problems. I leaned towards the window. Below, jungle as far as I could see. The plane rocked and jolted, falling a few hundred feet. The pilot leaned round grinning, Sorry mate, storm ahead, we should make it, if not we'll put down in Zindawa. I nodded. Parts of the land were still unexplored, there was so much potential. In the distance, beyond the Jirian range, heavy black clouds seethed with the light of a vast storm. The plane banked and we flew in the opposite direction. The pilot shouted, Slight diversion mate, we don't want to be over there. I nodded again. Leaning back in the seat, I felt the sweat dripping down my face. I took two mouthfuls of whisky from the flask, followed by a long drink from the water bottle. Twilight came fast, the sky flaming red then dark blue. I dozed.

A shout interrupted a dream of fly fishing in Scotland, Nearly there. I rubbed my eyes. We were circling. Port Campbell below, capital of the northern region, just a few shacks and a hotel. Towns meant nothing here. Three dirt roads to nowhere, a vast blackness beyond, and the river, its source in the western highlands. Far to the south, the sky periodically lit up like a huge theater. We landed, bumping heavily a couple of times. I thanked the pilot and staggered out of the plane. A huge figure was walking towards me. Caruthers? Yes, I replied. Name's Brodrick, Moss Brodrick. We shook hands. You're lucky to be here. The storm, he added, Should arrive tonight. We climbed into the jeep.

We sat in my room, the fan creaking above us, outside a torrent of rain. Be like this for a few hours, said Brodrick, Nothing else to do but down more of these. He pointed at the beer. Well, I suppose we'll have to make the best of it, I said. We sat in silence, the heat rendering all movement absurd. So Marshall, how did he die? I asked. Brodrick exhaled smoke, handing me another bottle, It was a game. A game? Yes, he continued, Christmas Day, they were playing a game. Who? I interrupted. Oh, some planters and Harry Morgan, he's a local trader, well, he drinks a bit you know, and they like to rib him now and then. That night they were putting a dead snake on his car roof, and when old Harry left the bar to drive home of course he saw the snake. So he dashed back into the bar yelling about a snake on his car. Everyone laughed and said, You're drunk old man, seeing things again. Marshall nipped outside and removed the snake, so when everyone went to see what Harry was on about naturally there was no snake. Harry had one more for the road, Marshall put the snake back, and the same thing happened, Harry came running in again scared out of his wits. They repeated the joke several times until Harry was frantic. The last time Marshall went out to remove the dead snake to give Harry a rest, there was a real snake, it bit him. Northern Taipan, must've fallen from a tree. He was dead within minutes. They thought it was his heart till they saw the fang marks, unmistakable. Poor old Marshall. And it finished off Harry, he left for England. Good God, I said. Brodrick turned and stared through the window at the rain, Yes, most unfortunate. By the way, this might slow us down, but things should clear. I suggest we get some rest, you must be exhausted. Good idea, I agreed. Stay in the room, he added, Keep the door locked, and here, take this. He handed me a .45. Haven't seen one of these since the war, I said. Where were you? he asked. North Africa mainly, how about you? Sweat dripping down his face, he stared, Burma, then here. He waved and closed the door. I washed, climbed onto the rickety bed, and fell asleep lulled by the crashing of the rain, the .45 on the floor.

A knock on the door. I touched the gun, Who's there? A deep voice, Big Man him wanna you eat breakfast. Footsteps down the corridor. The rain had stopped. I opened the blinds. Dawn, the end of the storm, retreating clouds penetrated by daggers of light. The air reeking of hot soggy vegetation. I could see the blue lines of the highlands a hundred miles to the north. A rooster pecked at the mud.

Brodrick was seated in the dining room, drinking tea. I hope you'll forgive me, I already ate, hope you slept well. Thank you, I said, Like a log. Master

Number One ready now, Brodrick shouted suddenly. A hulking native emerged from the kitchen. He placed a plate on the table and served a four inch Witches Grub, fried to perfection. Looks good, I said. This wallah fine man, said Brodrick. The native grinned and bowed. Well, dig in old chap, then I'll fill you in on what's happening. Good idea, I mumbled. I chewed the soft meat, relishing the smoky aftertaste. Brodrick lit a cigarette, inhaling deeply. It's very simple. Every member of the tribe wants a bungalow, a lawn, some gardening equipment, especially lawnmowers, and money to invest. I want the best for them, I hate to see them lose out, they helped us in the war you know. I recommended five hundred pounds each. Should see them through, they're all dead by forty anyway. Marshall was very against it for some reason. Is that all? I asked. Yes, Brodrick replied, You need to drive up country with me and sign with the chief. I'll be there, of course, you wouldn't make it alone. The missionaries send volunteers but they eat them. Nice fat missionary roasting on a fire. Have you ever seen that? No, I replied, Never. You get used to it, said Brodrick, First ate human in the war, thought it was monkey till they told me it was Jap, liver's the best part. Why do they leave you alone? I asked. Brodrick laughed softly, I'm the beer man, Imperial Breweries. I bring their beer, manna from heaven. We brew extra strong lager especially for them, sold nowhere else. Keeps them happy. It's currency, they treat it like gold. You know what they say? No, I said. He watched me, searching for signs of unease, Strong man strong beer. Come on let's get going, we must be back before night.

The village was a three hour drive through an emerald landscape, the grass lush with the recent rains. Trees laden with fruit, insects, brightly colored butterflies the size of dinner plates. Birds of Paradise. Brodrick was right, I could not have done the journey alone. We passed tribesmen carrying spears, naked except for penis horns, bones through their noses, their bodies muscled like Greek statues. Very few whites had ever been this far. They watched suspiciously until they saw Brodrick, then they cheered, running alongside the jeep mile after mile. We were towing a trailer crammed with beer. By the time we reached the village, sixty or seventy warriors surrounded us. Brodrick stopped the jeep and yelled, Where is Big Man One Talk? Take me to One Talk Big Man. The tribe sighed as one, a vast exhalation, as a very old man was lifted towards us on a chair, carried by six men their hard bodies caked in gray ash. One Talk Big Man me lug beer, Brodrick ranted, Strong man beer for big men. The old man gestured towards me, What name belong him? This man Master Number One, him Big Man too, friend of King. Pressed by the tribe, we followed the old chief to the long house, the interior lit by a single animal fat candle that sputtered in the breeze, the yellow light flickering over hundreds of skulls lining the walls. For a long time Brodrick lapsed into pidgin, the old man nodding occasionally, then he produced a document with the King's seal. All in order, he whispered, You just sign. I duly scrawled the quill over the parchment. Now we give them the beer and we leave. We want to be well away before nightfall.

I smoked a cigarette while warriors unloaded the beer. Brodrick stood while other warriors presented him with gifts, a twelve foot dead cobra, piglets, young girls, mirrors, a pack of cards. I stared across the countryside imagining the mine in a few years, the biggest in the world, and it would be ours. Poor old Marshall would be have been pleased. Pity about the view, but there was plenty more land, heavens, we'd only just started exploring the place. The Japs had tried to take it and now it was ours, we'd got there before the Americans. Who knows what lay beyond? If they wanted bungalows, lawns, lawnmowers, a few hundred pounds, they'd bloody well have them. I watched a group of monkeys in some nearby trees. A dominant male was pursuing younger members of the troop. Fitzroy's Macaques, said Brodrick, following my gaze, That one's the Big Man. Sometimes, I wonder what the hell we're doing, he continued, Damn pity how it's all going to change, with the mine, I was really quite attached. There's bags more land, I replied, You can always move up country if you want. But the monkey's aren't giving up their trees for bungalows and lawnmowers, are they? he interrupted, And they couldn't care less about gold. I stared at him, Don't be absurd man, of course not, they're dumb animals.

Six months later they filmed the opening of the mine, the excavations a gaping red hole in the earth. The gold was already starting to flow. The company's stock quadrupled, and I was promoted to head office. And the natives have tasted the fruits of their success, droned the narrator's BBC voice, Only a year ago these people were living in tribal poverty but today they enjoy a wealth which is the envy of anyone, all thanks to the Imperial Consolidated Mining Company. We saw a man naked except for his penis horn mowing a lawn by a bungalow. One of his wives was grinning at the camera, wearing nothing more than an apron. The narrator continued, It's a lovely day, and Mrs. Bangalooloo's off to do the shopping, the first supermarkets are on their way.

Eric Tessier

SATORI IN QUEBEC

The Fourniers arrived this morning in the province of Quebec, in the heart of what was once called *La Nouvelle France*. They just spent a month in Ontario, and after Toronto, a typical North-American city according to a French eye, Quebec City looks like home to them. In fact, it is neither *new* or *old* France, it is simply home. To be more precise, it looks like Saint-Malo, in Brittany, where Vincent Fournier's grandmother was born and raised.

The urban conception that has determined its topography is undeniably French. The streets of Toronto are long straight avenues that form a large checkerboard. On the contrary, the Quebecker ones, in the old town, are all in curves and bends, going up and down in a jumble, where the notion of East, West, South and North is useless. They are so narrow that they become a total nightmare for big cars like Chryslers, Pontiacs or Chevrolets, all vehicles conceived for right angle and large roadways.

Since he is strolling on the wooden floor of the Dufferin Terrace, Vincent Fournier has a strange feeling, which has nothing to do with the recovering of his cultural marks or with the common phenomenon of false reminiscence one sometimes feels in an unknown place. It is much deeper than that.

He was watching the St. Lawrence River when, all at once, he has been hit by a furious flow of images in which he discovered himself as a child rushing down the Casse-Cou staircase to get back home.

Home?

Where? Here?

Now?

In the hot summer of 2003 or... in a snowy evening of the 18th century? Dazed, he turns his head to face the Chateau Frontenac, comes back for a second to reality. He closes his eyes, dazzled by the sun at its zenith, sits down on a bench, trying to recompose himself. But the images continue to overflow his brain with childhood memories. Imaginary memories. For he has never lived in this city, has never been this young hungry boy running through a winter night, longing for a hot split pea soup. Breathless and worried by the vision of a sturdy woman – his mother - waiting for him behind a frosty windowpane. Anxious. Maybe a bit annoyed because he should be back from school by this time.

He glances at the Terrace, watches the families that saunter along, and a few kids who run and shout while playing a boisterous police and thief game. Two elderly persons who walk slowly, carefully, lost in their thoughts. A young girl on a bicycle whose dress flutters gently as her legs move and a rogue mild breeze blows.

A life is taking hold of him, a life that may have been his and whose reality is undeniable but foolish. Quebec City comes to him, at one and the same time insistent and modest, like an old friend who's wondering if he has been forgotten or not.

His mother doesn't like him hanging about the street after dark. October in Quebec is the season when people begin to stay more inside than outside. At night the town is deserted, the weather severe. The inhabitants eat and go to bed early, in the warmth of the roaring fires.

He is seven years of age. Maybe a little more. Did he come back from school? From church? Has he been buying something or calling on a friend? He can't tell but, one thing is sure, he is late.

- Mom will be angry, he figures.

Someone sits beside him on the bench. Absent minded, he moves a bit to give a seat to the new comer. A laugh. A fragrance. *Mademoiselle de Chanel.* Two sparkling green eyes. A charming and lovely lady is watching him.

- I can't believe it! She notices. Apart from the fact he looks much more intelligent than you, you are my husband's double.

Vincent restrains his laughter.

- Indeed? And where is this lucky guy?

- I don't know, he left me when I went shopping. Just because shopping bores him. What a nerd!

- This is a case of mental torture, you should get divorced as soon as possible.

She smiles, joyful.

- Is that what you think? She asks.

- Well, it's worth thinking about. But he sure doesn't deserve a loving wife like you.

She pouts.

- Oh, he is not so bad, he has his good side. And... (She gets closer to murmur what seems to be a secret) there's the girls.

He answers the same way.

- The girls?

She points out two teenagers who are looking at the landscape from the Terrace.

- These two are our daughters.

Vincent chuckles.

- You're kidding! This can't be.

- No? And why, if I may ask?

They're facing each other, eyes in eyes.

- A young woman like you can't have two children of this age. Tell me the truth, they're your sisters, uh?

She taps his forearm slightly.

- Oh no, you cheat, she exclaims. It's not fair, what can I answer to that?

Vincent guffaws.

- So, do you admit, Mrs Fournier, that I, Vincent Fournier, have won the game?

She stares at him, with a pitiless eye.

- No, I don't.

- What a bad loser you are!

- No, I'm not. Your compliment was far too exaggerated to be credible.

He approaches his lips from her ear and whispers:

- I see, in fact you can't resist it and you want me to repeat it.

- No...

She puts her arm around his neck, hesitates, then says:

- Yes, but it doesn't mean that I admit anything.

- Of course, dear.

*

- Be that as it may, I have found everything that I needed, Caroline Fournier remarks.

- You needed something and didn't tell me? I must be dreaming.

Caroline shrugs her shoulders and, for the first time, Vincent notices the parcels she is carrying with her.

- We have a family and some friends, if you remember, she explains. And as we are abroad, all these people are expecting us to bring back some souvenirs. In a way, I have worked this afternoon...

- Caroline, you work to earn money, not to spend it in a few horrid tourist traps.

- A few horrid traps! These beautiful Indian jewels? Oh! I should say *Ameridian* jewels. That's how the Quebecker name the Native Americans. And see this Inuit pipe. Your father will love it. Did you know *Eskimo* was a pejorative name? So they change it to *Inuit*.

Quietly, Caroline's voice fades away. Vincent quickened his pace, although he slips in the snow. His gloves are wet and his fingers frozen. So are his feet. For a second, he turns his face to the sky, opens his mouth, gulps a white flake. His throat is burning and he coughs. If he's sick, mom will tell him off.

- Vincent.

- Yes...

... wipes his hand on his coat...

- Yes mom.

- It's me, Caroline. Are you okay?

... sneezes again...

- Caroline?

She puts her palm on his torso, contracts her long and elegant fingers.

- You weren't listening to me, she states while examining him attentively. He feels she is really anxious. Smiles to put her mind at rest.

- I was listening to you, darling, but sometimes I love the melody so much that I can't hear the lyrics.

Caroline's nails scratch his nape.

- It isn't funny, Vince. You are as white as a sheet.

- What's going on? A little voice interrupts.

- Nothing Julie. Your father has just felt faint but it's over now. Where's your sister?

Julie, the Fournier's youngest daughter, looks at her father, stands on tiptoe to see him better.

- Are you going to die, daddy? She asks without any apparent emotion.

- No, Vincent answers, your mother overestimates my illness. I have nothing at all.

Caroline gazes at him like a nurse ready to reprimand a disobedient boy.

- Julie, where is your sister?

- Here she is. She was lacing her shoe.

- What's the matter? Laetitia steps in.

- Dad is supposed to die.

- Yes? So, dad, don't forget you promised to give me your skis, Laetitia says. Did you write this on your testament? If he didn't, you'll be my witness, Julie.

Vincent Fournier throws up his hands, casts a reproachful glance at Caroline.

- I'm not quite certain I like the way your daughters talk.

- You gave *our* daughters your silly sense of humor, Vince. Usually, you are rather proud of that, aren't you?

*

She has heard him walking in the staircase and has opened the door before he arrived on the landing. He doesn't see her face but there is no doubt: this reassuring robust figure is his mother. All of a sudden, he is no more a hero, no more a captain of the Royal Guards nor a trapper in the North, but a little boy, just a frightened little boy, who feels like going out of a sea of darkness, out of a cold ocean where revolting monsters slide between his legs, bite his skin, suck his blood. Horrified, he jumps step by step, faster and faster, arms wide open to catch his mother's body, to feel the loving warmth of her breast, of her hands, of her lips. He jumps, twists his ankle, falls down on the floor. Cries.

He has nothing, nothing but his age and the desire of being pressed against the body he comes from and should have never quit. Never! His mother caresses his hair, he snorts in her shoulders.

- Mom, mom... Oh MOM!

She hums a lullaby – It's all right, *mon enfant*, it's all right. *Maman t'aime*.

*

The siren of a boat tears the air over the St. Lawrence River. Seated on the balcony of his hotel room, Vincent Fournier is contemplating the town. He is serene. The images have disappeared but he understands he has experienced something rare, something that will count in his life, some sort of revelation deeply tattooed forever in his inner being. He does not know exactly what it's been. Neither what it'll bring him. But he knows that a curtain has been half-opened, that he has encountered briefly the mystery of life and its resolution. And that he is just one link in the chain of generations, but also the whole world itself, every single man and woman who live, has lived and will live. One and all. Past, present and future at the same time. From the birth of mankind till the end of time... And he feels at peace with himself, with life and death. Happy.

While Quebec City seems to stretch and purr like a cat in the sunshine of this lovely Canadian summer evening.

Floriana Hall

THE UNIVERSAL WORD

I had always dreamed of seeing Europe, and that dream came true in 1984. My husband, Bob, had promised me when we were married in 1948 that he would take me to see Italy and Switzerland someday. He had served in Italy during World War II and loved that area. He also enjoyed Switzerland and Lake Como where he enjoyed rest and relaxation days.

The realization of that dream came about partly because our youngest son, Robert, was working for American Airlines as a purchasing agent.˙We were allowed seven free trips a year. After checking out several tour agents, we decided to take the Trafalgar Tour of seven countries which was reasonably priced.

We prepared for the trip by obtaining passports, exchanging U. S. Dollars for a few country's currencies, studying pertinent phrases in each language, and packing one suitcase each. What we weren't prepared for were the toilets in Europe!

We flew to Dallas in September and visited Robert and his family before boarding the plane to London. After arriving at Gatwick airport at six A.M. And going through customs, we took a taxi to our hotel. Since we had jet lag, Bob and I slept for three hours, and then walked around the area., where we bought fruit at an open air market. That evening, we watched some TV, and remarked that British commercials were very funny. The facilities at the hotel were adequate, but we were amused at finding the flush on top of the toilet. There was a teapot provided, so I made some tea, which is always relaxing.

It was time to retire. There were two single beds with metal frames at the head and foot of the beds. Although I rarely have nightmares, I woke up in the morning dreaming that I was chained to the bed. My feet were dangling over the metal frame.

The next morning, after a Continental breakfast of delicious pastries, we took the subway downtown to see London's sights, Big Ben, Buckingham Palace, Trafalgar Square, and the Tower of London. We missed the changing of the guard at the palace, but did see the Royal Horsemen rounding the entrance to the palace. Walking along the River Themes, I marveled at some of the architecture.

The following morning we met the forty-eight fellow passengers on the tour. It was a congenial group of tourists from the United States, Australia, England, and South Africa. Our tour guide, Maria, was Portuguese by birth, but lived in the United States. The bus driver, Luke, lived in Belgium.

The bus took us past the beautiful White Cliffs of Dover, where we boarded Townsend Thoresen Spirit boat and crossed the English Channel to Calais, France, and on to Paris. It was in Paris that we encountered what was to be a series of mishaps connected with bathroom facilities.

We had stopped at McDonald's on the way to Paris, and, of course, found the bathrooms without a problem, except the women had to wait in lines for at least twenty minutes. The men were able to get in and out in time to buy a hamburger, etc., so Bob bought my lunch. Otherwise, because of the time wasted waiting, I may not have had time to buy anything to eat. We stopped at Montmarte, viewed the city from Sacred Heart Church, passed the Arc de Triumph, and stopped at the Eiffel Tower and Notre Dame Cathedral.

At the hotel, I intended to take a bath before retiring, but couldn't find the bathtub faucet — there was none on the bathtub. However, after cautiously turning all the knobs on the sink, water began flowing into the tub from underneath the soap dish on the side of the sink. The flush for the commodes everywhere in Europe were always hard to locate. Some pulled up, some pulled down, and some couldn't be found. The beds in the tiny room were so small that our mattresses slid halfway to the floor as we awakened.

Every hotel and its bathroom facilities were a challenge. Finding a toilet when the bus stopped was rather easy, though, because everyone in Europe knew the word toilet or toilette. Except when there wasn't any.

In Italy, Maria told Bob to relieve himself behind a canvas if he couldn't find a toilet. Bob kept walking until he found a bar with a crude so-called toilet that had a cord to pull down cord to flush.

Most of the lavatories in Italy had older women as attendants who expected to be tipped. They earned their living in that manner. Not being familiar with the coins caused me some problems. Nevertheless, I usually paid after using the facility, so that I had time to think, for I was always in a rush to get to the toilet.

One gray haired little old lady gave me the evil eye when I zoomed past her to the booth. It was filled with sewage and rags, but I was desperate to relieve myself. While I was in the process, someone started pounding on the door. I said "Wait a minute, please," and then proceeded to open the door to find two young women who evidently thought they couldn't wait. As I passed the attendant, I put a coin into her dish and indicated that the toilet was messy, messy. She looked surprised, and to my amazement, returned the coin.

In Venice, a male attendant smiled and sprayed a disinfectant as I entered, so I tipped him generously. Venice was a wonderful city to see while cruising in gondolas along the canals. It was romantic listening to the accordionist playing and singing enchanting Italian love songs.

One of our fellow travelers didn't believe in tipping and experienced a rather frightening incident in Rome. As she entered the stall, she waved at the woman in charge, who immediately rushed after her, and unsuccessfully tried to push open the door. The woman began screaming and shouting, pounding on the door, and subsequently all the other doors. She literally went berserk.

Another tourist has a happier occurrence. As she entered the toilet, a sweet little lady smiled, wiped off the seat, and motioned to her to enter. She received an adequate tip.

While in Rome, we saw the Vatican, St. Peter's and Michaelangelo's Sistine Chapel and walked along the same streets Roman soldiers had walked ages before. I felt fulfilled seeing Rome's magnificent sights. However, the traffic there was horrendous, and one driver who tried to cut the bus off, got into an argument with Maria, and called her unmentionable names. Bob, who knew some Italian unmentionables himself, walked out of the bus and confronted the driver, who left immediately when he saw Bob's six feet two stature.

Probably the most difficult rest room to find was in Switzerland. I was shopping in a modern department store when I suddenly had terrible stomach cramps. After asking for directions to the women's rest room, I used the elevator and passed through a maze of storage sections filled with mannequins before I found it. Once there, the trouble started. Of all the toilets in Europe, it seemed as though the flushes were deliberately placed so that the user can't find them. There was no flush anywhere in that room, not on top, or on the side, or on the wall, overhead, or on the floor. I spent ten minutes looking for one and never did find it. How embarrassing, the one place I needed and attendant, there was none.

Switzerlanhd was lovely, though, riding an incline to the top of the Alps, and viewing the simplicity of the quaint homes with flower boxes on the windows, and cows in the meadows with bells on their necks. The view from the top was spectacular.

In Austria, we stayed at a Bed & Breakfast. The beds were built for short people, and Bob had to sleep in a fetal position all night while I trudged down the hall several times to a common bath room.

We stopped in Munich and drove through Germany's Black Forest. One young passenger was experiencing diarrhea, so Luke had to stop often to accommodate him. However, after I gave him a Kaopectate table, his agony soon stopped.

Without a doubt, the worst so-called toilet of all was in Amsterdam. The city has such historic beauty, canals, and narrow buildings where pianos are hoisted up to rooms from the outside. We stopped in a bar and asked for a rest room, which, to my dismay, was a hole in the middle of the floor. What could I do? I had complained previously that the toilet paper, called "Softie," felt like sandpaper, but now there was no toilet and no paper.

Holland and Belgium were lovely with tulips in full bloom, windmills and many canals. Luke drove by his home to show us where he lived.

Before we were dropped off at our respective hotels in England, the bus was blocked by a car in the center of an alley. Bob and another sturdy man got out of the bus to pick up the small car and move it to the side so we could pass by. There was a mix-up in our reservations at our hotel, but we were driven by taxi to another one at one o'clock in the morning. The new room had a very uncomfortable bed, and a shower without a shower curtain, and a stopped-up drain. Needless to say, the bathroom was literally flooded after we had taken our shower.

Upon leaving the bus, Maria told all the tourists that our tour was one of the best she had ever guided, with friendly and agreeable passenger. That made everyone feel very good.

I didn't even mind the bees in Florence, Italy, chasing us, or going up the wrong way on a one way street in Rome, or waiting extra long for two teens to return to the bus several times, or even the poorest toilet facilities, for the trip was a dream fulfilled. It was memorable despite the toilets, and funny, because of them. I think Thomas Crapper, who invented the toilet, would have had a good laugh, too.

Jim Ganley

SEASONS OF THE LAKE

Leaving home was perhaps the most challenging thing I have ever had to do. It was Halloween, 2002, and as I sat in the back yard on my children's old swing set, I was overwhelmed by a plethora of vivid images from the past. I could remember carrying my children around the yard on my shoulders when they were babies, trying to quell their crying, setting up their swing set and encouraging my three-year-old daughter, Sarah, as she tried to jump to grab the trapeze bar only to fall down time and time again. She eventually went on to become a standout basketball player in middle school. I remember sliding down a homemade bobsled run with my son Joey when he was only three. When he tried to go it alone, he went airborne like a cruise missile and scared himself silly. There were baseball games and badminton tournaments in our back yard I helped Sarah develop her pitching skills for softball. Joey, at age two, drove his tricycle off a cliff and into the gully behind our house. Then there was Joey at age three, going down the driveway standing up on his plastic toboggan singing 'Surfer Joe'. He never fell once. When he was eight, I taught him to skateboard down our newly paved road as his friends stood around watching with respectful silence. As I said, the move from home was difficult for me. And if I tend to ruminate about this more than some of you would like, just try to understand; this could just as well have been you.

Divorce! This is something that I had always assumed happened to others, not to me. I had planned my marriage and family with meticulous detail, never considering the possibility that my wife of nearly twenty years would leave me for another man...the Sunday School teacher at our church. This was beyond my comprehension. The temporary court order pursuant to my impending divorce ordered me out of my home where I had lived since 1985. Worse yet, my business, a private exercise training practice, would need to be moved as well. It took perhaps two weeks, but eventually I replied to an advertisement in the local paper and found what appeared to have been a suitable domicile overlooking the shores of Lake Massabesic in Auburn, New Hampshire. This was nearly twenty miles away from my home in Bow.

Serving as the water supply for the city of Manchester, New Hampshire, Lake Massabesichas was spared many of the problems of urbanization. Swimming and water skiing there are not permitted, and the 42 Sq. mile watershed area surrounding the lake has been off limits to development for decades. Massabesic has a 28-mile shoreline. Consequently, it is easy to understand why the early New Hampshire residents would have been drawn here for an escape from the city. In fact, Lake Massabesic had been so popular that trolley lines had made regular runs from Manchester proper. In many ways, it was another time and another place. Massabesic straddles the town of Auburn and the City of Manchester, yet the lake area has retained its rural character, setting it apart from the inner city environment of nearby Manchester. Located in the southern part of New Hampshire in northern New England, Lake Massabesic received its name from the Penacook Indians and means "Place of Much Water," in their Algonquin dialect. Topographically Lake Massabesic is comprised of two large bodies of water separated by Route 28 at Deer Neck Bridge, which divides it into Front Pond to the East and Back Pond to the West. Ultimately, the lake drains into the Merrimack River via Cohas Brook.

My landlord for this property on Lake Massabesic was named David, a man whose claim to fame was that he was the cousin of a U.S. Senator and nephew of a former N.H. Governor. David did not like to deal with the public and, instead, all communication was via his wife and surrogate, Patricia. David and Patricia lived in the sort of large, ostentatious compound resembling a ski lodge which one would find in a place like Aspen, Colorado. Their driveway was at least a quarter of a mile long. The grounds were meticulously groomed with rolling hills going all the way down to the Massabesic shoreline. It featured a man-made pond stocked with gold fish as well as an "industrial grade" tennis court. Patricia stipulated that I lease the place for one year for $1,500 a month. She also requested references, and all of them were contacted. I must have passed muster with this odd couple, for several days later I was invited back to their compound and offered a leasing agreement to sign. By temporary court order Joey, age 12, would be staying at the lake with me from Wednesday until Sunday evenings. My daughter Sarah, 15, had the same option, but for reasons of her own chose to stay with her mother in our Bow homestead.

My new home was nice. The structure itself was a rather large, rectangular building...very old, probably a winterized cottage dating back to the early 1900s, though recently modernized and enlarged. The kitchen was about three times larger than what I needed, but this was certainly no problem at all. The living room was framed by large, roughly hewn oak beams and offset by white ceilings and walls. Of course, a great sound system, was mandatory, and I often found myself wishing I could have had a place like this when I was 25. The basement was a complete disaster. It had served as a stable at one point. Filled with decades worth of junk, access to it was from the outside by way of a large, barn door. My personal training business was forced out of my original home and this would have to serve as its new location. I went to work on the place with a vengeance, cleaning the dust, laying down several coats of concrete sealant. I also lay down carpet and installed mirrors. At this point, it was beginning to look like a gym... a tad rough around the edges perhaps, but a gym none the less.

Because my monthly expenses had more than tripled, I all too quickly found myself needing more clients to keep the business solvent. I began exploring the option of doing telephone consultations as a means of generating more revenue. Fortunately, many of my clients followed me to my remote lakeside location.

The very first weekend after I had moved in, Joey became a little homesick and wanted to go home to work on his models. We arrived back at our home in Bow at a little after 8 p.m. on Saturday and, son of a gun, my wife's married boyfriend's car was parked in the driveway. By the way, my soon to be ex was the choir director at our church and her paramour was a Sunday School teacher there. The pastor of the church, believe it or heave it, was aware of what had been going on, but lacked the testicular fortitude to speak to them about the immorality of their choices. This was such a poor example to set for our children.

"I can't go in there, Joe," I explained, "because if I do there's no telling what may happen, and I don't want to go to jail!"

Although Joe decided to go inside to play with his models, he had no problems demanding that the boy friend leave. I once wrote that the only genuine tough guys I know are dead. I guess I was wrong.

The overwhelming sense of solitude in my lakeside abode was difficult for me. When Joey was there, everything was fine. When he was not I had to fight against sinking into a deep depression. It seemed as if in light of what I had personally experienced, fathers were irrelevant and that marriage was a sham. I was certain that the complete collapse of our society was only a decade or so away. Frustrated beyond belief, I toyed briefly with fleeing to Canada or, as an option of last resort, suicide. However, I truly believed that my children needed me. My job as a parent, was not yet finished, and I needed to do whatever was necessary to see both of my children to a healthy, productive adulthood. For hours at a time, I would sit at my computer contemplating the meaning of life and ultimately developing a sense of kinship with Henry David Thoreau, who had spent a year at Walden Pond in nearby Massachusetts. Although one hundred and fifty years earlier, Thoreau had written that most men lead lives of quiet desperation. However, I was not about to allow despair to overwhelm me. By now, I was angry and vowed to fight to save my family.

First, I would need to save myself by implementing an effective, nondestructive way to manage the stress of my coming divorce and isolation from my family. I did this by immersing myself in vigorous exercise. I lifted weights in my gym, ran around the lake at dawn, and hiked the surrounding trails in the evening. It was autumn, and as I strode over the circuitous miles of rugged paths winding their way along the Massabesic shoreline, my senses were overwhelmed by the explosion of colors; the reds, golds, yellows, and purples of the foliage highlighted by the setting sun, contrasted sharply with the deep blue of the sky as the water lapped softly against the rocks on the shore. The wildlife was abundant. There were deer, moose, fox, coyotes, rabbit, and fisher cats, as well as red-tailed hawk, osprey, barred owl, and great blue heron. I surmised that we all, that is, the wildlife and I, were playing a part in a cosmic play whose author or playwright lay hidden away from scrutiny.

Through all of this, like an ever present sentinel, was the lake. It seemed almost as if it was a character in a novel with a personality of its own. Lake Massabesic had been here before the arrival of the first Europeans, in fact, before the advent of the Woodland Penacooks, or the archaic peoples who had preceded them. The lake would be here long after we were gone as a master time keeper and impartial observer.

It was while on one of my early morning jaunts around the lake that I thought of Passaconaway, Chief of the Penacooks, whose legend and historical persona are difficult to separate. In 1627, Passaconaway had founded the Penacook Confederation, uniting all of the regional Abenaki as a means of confronting the Mohawk. Prior to his death, he had advised his tribesmen that many more Europeans would be coming and that the Penacooks should make peace with them. The other information about Passaconaway is more suspect. It was said that he could turn dead leaves green, make water burn, rocks move, trees dance, and change himself into a burning man. His death, so the legend tells us, took place as he was paddling his canoe across Massabesic on his way to Cohas Brook. A great wind and accompanying white caps with great fog suddenly arose on the lake, sweeping Passaconaway away into the afterlife. This is a legend in many ways similar to those of Jesus and Mohammed.

Strange though it may seem, I actually thought that I could sense Chief Passaconaway's presence as I traversed the length and breadth of Lake Massabesic's shores. I wondered what sage advice he could possibly offer me.

The seasons, we have been told, were held sacred by ancient peoples, with each having a character of its own. . .a metaphor for life. What follows is a brief synopsis of the "vision quest' I experienced in each of the four seasons during my tenure at Lake Massabesic.

Autumn 2002

My initial sense here was one of deep relaxation. However, there was also the sense of loss when my daughter Sarah chose to stay with her mother. It has been said that if one were to drop a frog into a vat of boiling water that the frog would hop out immediately. If, however, that frog was dropped into a vat of water at room temperature and the water was gradually brought to a boil, that frog would stay in the vat until parboiled to death. Metaphorically speaking, I might have been that second frog, though it was not until now that I came to the realization.

Most alarming of all during this time was an event that took place at Eagle Rock on Massabesic. A granite promontory overlooking most of the lake, Eagle Rock was supposed to have been a place held sacred by the Penacooks. It was on a Sunday afternoon in late November that Joe and I hiked there. On a whim, I had chosen to invoke the intercession of the deity for help in resolving our problems. At the pinnacle of Eagle Rock, and with my son Joey watching, I raised my arms and prayed to The Great Spirit for help in saving my marriage and family. The water below was a deep blue. Off in the distance the setting sun cast a bright pathway across the lake to the base of Eagle Rock. Joey looked at me and wondered whether or not my plea had been heard. "Ask God to give us a sign that he heard us," he told me. So I did.

"Hey, God!" I shouted, "Give us a sign that we've been heard!" In an instant, we could see tree tops in the distance heaving violently back and forth. White caps appeared in the water far below, and not long after that Eagle Rock was struck by a powerful wind that nearly knocked Joey and me off of Eagle Rock altogether. I can still recall telling him, "Be careful what you ask for, Joe, because you just might get it!"

Winter 2002-03

The snow arrived early that winter and it kept on snowing nearly two or three times a week until the following April. Besides the weather, the greatest challenge here was the structural integrity or lack thereof of the house in which we were residing. For starters the roof leaked. Worse yet, the porous concrete that comprised the basement walls leaked as well, necessitating that I shovel a trench around the foundation. I also had to shovel the roof after each and every snow storm. I used an ax to break up the ice dams lining the edge of the roof. The driveway and walkways had to be shoveled as well. This was the worst winter in terms of snowfall in recent memory. Early one Saturday morning as I was up on the roof in the midst of a prodigious snow removal project. I was hit in the back of my head by a snowball. From the laughter I knew in an instant that Joey had been the perpetrator. Armed with a shovel, he volunteered to give me a hand. It was at this point that I realized that as detrimental as the divorce proceedings may have been, this court ordered living arrangement had actually facilitated a better relationship between the two of us.

For every negative there is a balancing, positive component. This was true in my life and it was also true with the heavy snowfall, which created ideal conditions for snow shoeing. Joe and I went off on various cross-country treks on our snowshoes, which received more usage that winter than in any other year since I had purchased them in 1977. After one of our snow shoe excursions, as I was driving Joe home on a Sunday night, the following conversation ensued:

"Hey, Joe...Have you been on any dates yet? You know...like with a girl?" Joe just shrugged and said, "Well...not exactly, Dad. Why are you asking?" "Well I... was thinking. I haven't dated anyone since I became seriously involved with your mother. With the way things have been developing, you and I will probably begin dating people in the not too distant future. In which case we'll be more like brothers than father and son. But I'll need to draw the line at us going out on double dates together." Joe and I both had a good laugh over that one.

Spring 2003

Ever Since I had moved into my lakeside residence in the fall, there had been a series of odd occurrences which logic could not explain. On more than one occasion my washing machine had started up on its own. Late at night I would be awakened by a loud crash in my basement followed by the sound of footsteps ascending a long staircase. The problem here was that there was no staircase leading from the basement to the house proper. On yet another night I was awakened by what at the time I thought was a motor vehicle accident. The next morning I entered my office to discover that the book shelves had been torn off the walls, my professional journals and text books had been strewn all over the office floor, and my computer had been turned on. I did not want to contemplate the source of this one at all. There were other less ominous events as well...two barred owls circling over my house late at night, one crying out "Hoo! Hoo! Hoo-Hoo!" and the other going "Haa! Haa! Haa-Haa!" While training a client in my basement gym at 9 a.m. on a Friday, she and I both heard what sounded like a child running from my living room and across the kitchen. I was shocked. "WHAT'S THAT?" Nonplused, my client just said, "Isn't that Joey". Quickly I explained that I had dropped my son off at school an hour and a half prior. "WAIT HERE!" I told her as I ran out the barn door, up, and into the house only to find that the place was empty. Yet, on my return to the gym, my client, now somewhat nervous, told me that as soon as I had run out the barn door that whatever we had heard had run back from whence it had come. Such events persisted. I got out of bed in the middle of the night on my way to obtain a drink of water when, in the dark of my kitchen I heard something behind me snarling like a rabid dog and causing the hairs on the back of my neck to come to attention. I turned the lights on only to find that no one was there.

As unsettling as the events which I have just described may have been, I had far more serious concerns with which to contend. First on the agenda was my divorce, heading for mediation some time in July. To have any chance at all I would need to prove to the court that I could obtain financing for my home and pay off my wife's share of the equity. The remainder of that spring found me hunting for financing and passing on documents to my attorney regarding my financial assets as well as evidence of my wife's illicit affair.

Summer 2003

It's 5 a.m., some time in early July and I'm running down Chester Road on my way into Auburn Village. Off in the distance I can hear the doleful calls of loons on the other side of the lake. Up ahead, a great blue heron resembling a prehistoric pterodactyl, launches itself from its nesting place near the road and flies low over the water, into a fog bank, and out of sight. As intriguing as these two preceding incidents may have been, I was lost in thought, still contemplating my rapidly approaching divorce.

By this point my life seemed to be finally falling into place. First of all, the court appointed guardian ad litem had come around 180 degrees, recommending that my son be allowed to live with me and that I be given our house contingent upon my ability to obtain financing. This had come about in response to Joe having told the guardian about the true nature of his mother's relationship with her boyfriend. While my quest for a stable home environment was moving ahead, my employment situation was far from that. Inquiries into what I could do to repackage myself and get hired had gone nowhere as well. Not long after this I was in my gym furiously pumping up my triceps with close grip bench presses. While it may have been over ninety degrees outside, my gym was freezing without any assistance from air conditioning. The mirrors were frosted. I could see my breath, and steam was radiating off my arms... definitely a strange scenario, however by now not all that unexpected. With the completion of my set, I racked the barbell and thought about all that I had experienced here. I think Nietzsche may have been on to something when he wrote, "That which does not kill me makes me stronger." If so, then by the time of my lakeside summer I had grown stronger than a wad of limburger cheese that had sat over night on a hot radiator.

A couple of weeks later I had been out hiking around the lake once more at sunset. My divorce had been finalized on July the 14th, Bastille Day. I stood on a small boulder above the water's edge as I watched the sun, appearing like a large, crimson ball sink slowly behind the trees along Massabesic's western shore. In my hands is a circular wreath of desiccated flowers, the wreath my bride had worn in her hair for our wedding. With neither fanfare nor emotion, I tossed it into the lake and watched as it was carried away by the current. Now my divorce was final.

Autumn 2003

By now I have come full circle. I have my home and custody of Joe. It's a Thursday and I'm driving my pickup truck back to Bow with a load of my personal belongings to begin the process of my move home. Ever since the divorce had been finalized, my ex-wife has had to rent this property from me until she could get situated in a new home of her own. I recall turning on to my street. Hey, Joe by Jimi Hendrix is on the radio and I can't wait to return. Pulling into my driveway, I jump from my truck, drop down on my knees, and kiss the ground. Home at last!

That Saturday afternoon I gazed out of my living room window and saw Joe sitting in the dirt across the street with sketchpad in hand. Going outside to investigate, I asked him what he was doing. Joe said not a word, but rather presented the sketch pad to me as if to seek my approval. Displayed thereon was a portrait of our home, my truck parked within the garage. Back Home said the portrait.

Louie Levy

THE NICKEL NYC '30S

I remember when ....

one Buffalo Nickel coin got us a big grilled kosher all beef hot dog at 'Nathans' Brooklyn Coney Island, hmmm, their mouth watering spiced garlic aroma could be smelled a mile away by every two and four legged hungry schnozzola alive. For chasers...there still ain't nothin' like real natural root beer, tap draft filled in a giant mug with sizzlin' foam, ticklin' ya nose. Oh yeah, Nathans french fries were also special made, scooped 'n salted to a big generous overflowing bag, their chunky crisp taste never dupe'd. Next door, was a big soft ice cream cone store, yep! just a nickel if ya had th' extra cents.

All that for 3 x 5 = 15cents, what heavenly scents ....? For the rest of our quarter savings, there was more fun ahead, Yep! Maybe ya guessed it, a sure stomach upset'r ride on the original wood framed Coney Island Roller Coaster 'Cyclone' and the spiraling fast 'Whip' rides. Electric BUMPer cars and screamin' happy kids. Who alive remembers Luna Steeple Chase Park? Ya gotta a million rides if ya had almost a buck! Many were original, now extinct and never dup'd ... long since, destroyed by fire.

Just in case, we always kept a dime in another pocket. That would take us round trip from home on the fun elevated subway. We always rode the front car that had a windshield window. Sadly, many of my kid camaraderie, and nostalgic 'Coney Island' have almost become an extinct place as I remember of my Brooklyn home town. Affordably, where so much could be enjoyed even when working for the minimum federal wage of 25cts an hour.

Not ever forgetting, the same each nickel 'Sum' total of the following treasures; Movies; 10+2cts tax, kids 5cts, for a triple feature show of a comedy, cowboy and a scary picture. My Dad told of times when 2 kids admitted for a nickel. The kids that had 2 looked for another that had 3 pennies, imagine that? Really BIG fat Hershey Mr. Chocolate Goodbars and all other favorite brands; ice cream pops and sugar cones. popcorn, big kosher sour barreled pickles, giant 12 oz Pepsi soda in cold bottles, potato knishes, etc. Neva we forgetta ....

of so much more ....

I'm now in tears, thinking that all of it was just for a then silvered nickel and soo goood. Five valuable, treasured real copper pennies. Bottle deposits were 2 and 5cts. If we was ever so lucky to find one thrown away, by some rich person.

While visiting from L.A. Ca later after arriving on a hot summer day during 2002 in Brooklyn, NY, I looked to treat my Granddaughter Maureen for my all time favorite refreshment. Nowhere could we find a candy store with a soda fountain. Finally, my seeing an outside newsstand, which was usually a sure sign, we found a parking space, having to shrink impossibly between cars. Now, we're almost gasping with thirst as we entered and confronted the less than, friendly, attending counter person.

"Could we please have 2 chocolate *egg creams and also, where are all the different kinds of cookies that are packed in bulk boxes usually placed in a rack?" I would have not dared to mention that they were just a penny and 2cts some 70 years ago. Appearing annoyed and his probably thinking I'm from another planet.

"Sorry Mista, he replied, this is NO a grocery store, NO that kinda *eggs, creams or cookies like you want, Icea cream ana soda in th'freeza over dere. "

My never bothering to explain to this strange accented foreigner from another time and unfamiliar cultural antiquity. We left with two badly flavored soda filled cans costing 95cts each with no clue as to whatever happened to the penny cookies and 5ct Ubet chocolate syrup egg creams of my own fond, youthful, and, memorable fun neighborhood times.

Those were some of the best cultural ghetto days of my life. How much fun it was when melting in the NY City pot together. We ate 'talian, polish, chinees, jewish, greek, soul foods and whatever we explored to discover was even more had when savin' allowances and errand tips. Someday, I'll tellya about Big Band sounds and teenage, slooow and jitter bugged dancing. Love petting was the greatest addictive high we sneaked out for.

Oh! yeah, who out there also remembers them little 6 for a quarter 'White Castle' onion/cheese ham burgers? An all night drive in, and we had tummy 'heaven' brought right to our car. They since went 'frozen packed' for LA now, as is my old, skippin' heart, similarly bein' frost felt about it all.

My also re-calling as teenagers, we bluntly made fun of any candy-store merchant who over charged us by our hollering...

"What crooks! they must even charge for th' water 'round here"!

Unbelievably for me and to those, many of my time, that have since come to reminisce...everywhere ... these 21st century, 5ct less, long since, passed away, unpolluted days.

Wondering, now, if we kids of the 30s were ever over heard and still now, bein' 'Crooked' for some fancy bottled french and fujee water...??

'n ...most all of the best, sadly gone ... unaffordably.

for worse ... and a lot less

'Coney Isle Nickel Fun.

*Chocolate Egg-Cream soda
Recipe;
Best *mixed in a tall wide-mouth coke type glass.*

add; a lot a 2-3oz of U-BET or Hershey dark Chocolate syrup- if ya like it sweeet mix equal amounts of whole cows milk with the syrup first. thenadd a fresh opened plain selzer (soda water) bottle, cherry flavored OK, Pour in slooowly while mixing kinda quickly. Watch-out for the errupting foam. Lips ready? Sip right away, enjoy, and please all ....

Respectfully 'toast' to my ole home town; 'Brooklyn', NYC

Maureen Audley

COLOSSEUM

We were unprepared for the great size of the Colosseum, despite having viewed it from close distances in the days before our visit. As we climbed the hill, it progressively took over our horizon, each step realising its volume. Our summit became its foothill. The sun behind it darkened its face, the features shadowed by a suggestion of menace. Unlike many of the other sights of Rome, where imagination must re-build the fallen and fragmented ruins, the first view of the Colosseum confirmed the past. But there was evidence also of the present in the trimmings of tourism littered around its circumference: the souvenir stall, the postcard sellers and, clasping their guide books and maps were the sightseers. There were the occasional clusters of guided tours, but most had come to see for themselves. The expressions of those sitting and laying at the perimeter were of the day's heat and the ungiving pavements they had walked. The clicks of the cameras competed with the horns of the traffic, now behind us. Ahead was the Colosseum.

Too much remained for the scars to matter. This was the theatre of gladiators, lions and Christians, exactly as we had been told. The division between fact and fiction was unimportant, real or imagined heroes would still know this as the place of their victories. Tiers of arches took the eye with the curve of the wall, the columns with its height. It's bulk was toned with artistry, its mass veneered with elegance. We passed under the main entrance archway, where darkness from overhead gave a temporary cooling.

In contrast the interior was an anticlimax. It was eroded. The size remained. The many people scattered around the arena emphasised the emptiness of the auditorium, designed to seat fifty thousand. It was decayed. Looking down where once the arena floor had been, the remaining walls of the underground corridors and rooms made little sense. Around the wall itself, the plan was confused. Time and later generations had stolen its identity. Time, less selective, had frayed only its edges. The Romans had stolen from its body. Little marble remained, leaving only bricks and stone.

We sat for a while before leaving, to rest and to know it should its name be mentioned in the future. Without the view of the destruction below, more order came to the sloping steps of seats above. The many entrances became a honeycomb of history. Across from us was a simple cross. We couldn't hear the sounds of battle, the roar of lions, the prayers of martyrs. But the massive wall muffled the noise of today's Rome and, in the stillness, maybe we did experience the expectation of that moment, just before a show begins.

NOTES ON CONTRIBUTORS

Alan Morgan was born in Cheltenham, England and educated at The Kings School in the cathedral city of Gloucester. He had many professions including banker, teacher, advisor. These poems speak of the emotional currents which shape our lives: happiness and sadness, hopes and desires. But most of all, of love. He now lives in the South of France.

Alice Parris is an award winner in the United Kingdom's Forwardpress Top 100 Poets of 2005 contest. Published in Cracked Lenses, Scorched Earth Publishing, Adiago Verse Quarterly, Asian American Poetry, Redwebz, Timbooktu, Taj Mahal Review, Explorers, Holistic Junction, Subtle Tea, AMAG, Sacramento Arts, Poetry & Music, and NISA. Her first book Soulgasm is available online and a audio version of Soulgasm is available at Tower Records, Cdbaby as well as digitally online. Ms. Parris' second book, Silenced Voices Speak is available through cyberwit.net. Lives in Arizona.

Andrew McIntyre lives in San Francisco. Recently, he has published stories in *Taj Mahal Review, Windhover, Gold Dust Magazine*, and *Children, Churches And Daddies Literary Magazine.*

Barbara Beck-Azar is an artist living now in Tucson, AZ; born into a traveling family, and continued that journey into adult life. "As an artist living in foreign land it opened my eyes to the diverse and beautiful ways cultures live and view their worlds totally outside what I had ever known. The world grew small as I saw similarities in each country and people. I discovered a vast wealth of knowledge through the countries history, spiritual beliefs and present way of life. Each country contains it's own beauty and I as an artist fell broadly in love with every place I lived... Everywhere was visual eye candy, and it seems like not enough time in eternity to paint all the wonders of this earth." *Email: amalgamarts@comcast.net*

Barbara Simcoe was born and raised in upstate New York and received an AA in Humanities from Corning Community College before transferring to S.U.N.Y., New Paltz, where she received a BS in Art Education. She moved west with her daughter, Heather, and lived in various cities in California. Three years ago, she relocated to Arizona. While in California, she received a certificate in Graphic Design from UC Davis Extension and she is currently working on a certificate in Interior Design from Sheffield in New York City (a home-study course). She has been painting in acrylics, watercolor and pastels for over 25 years and focuses on landscapes of the southwest. Her paintings are displayed and available for purchase on www.ArtWanted.com/BSimcoe. To purchase gift items displaying her work, please visit www.CafePress.com/SimcoeStudios. Also, visit www.artquest.com and see Barb's work, as well as others artists'. *Email: barbsimcoe@cox.net*

Ben Albares, photographer and Spanish graphic designer. From very young he travels on the way of the art experiencing diverse technical, he finds in the photography his great vocation. He has received several awards and at the moment he exposes his work around the world. *www.benalbares.net Email: benalbares@hotmail.com*

Bob Blackett (b. 1953): "BS Biology 1975, MS Biochemistry 1989, AAS Computer Programming 2001. Have worked numerous, varied positions. Currently in customer technical support for an ISP." *Email: abraxis29@hotmail.com*

Cher Peterson: "I am a professional archaeologist who also dabbles in photography. I currently have a website at www.artwanted.com/cher which features many of my images. I still work with 35 millimeter film cameras but have come into the digital world through Photoshop Creative Suite. My husband and I love to explore by either 4-wheeling into an area or backpacking (or both). We love to get away from the beaten track and go remote. My photography is oriented to landscape/outdoor images, where both exploration and discovery are highlighted. My three images of Death Valley National Park were taken in very remote areas of the park, where few people venture." *Email: Cpsh20@aol.com*

Cheri Carter from Texas is 58 years old, happily married and retired from mortgage banking. "My ambition is to be the world's oldest skydiver and to that end I run 4 miles every morning, teach Tai Chi and lift weights for strength twice a week. It requires a fair amount of strength to put on 40 pounds of gear and hang onto the outside of a jump plane in flight to launch a formation skydive. My plan is to ride my Yamaha to the drop zone on my 100th birthday, jump with my friends all day and brag about it all night." *Email: getcarter2@earthlink.net*

Darlene M. Nixon: "I have expressed by artistic talent in various manners over the years from coloring books to pen & ink to knitting, but have confined myself to oil painting in last couple of years. I have had my paintings in juried shows mainly in Colorado and in Oregon. I also have paintings in private collections." *www.chakragallery.com Email: idarmarnix@yahoo.com Tel. 303-986-0592*

David Miller is a world traveler and his photography has become an intricate part of his journeys. His travels have taken him from war torn Lebanon to dusty streets in rural Myanmar but in process his awe of this incredible world has only increased. May the journey continue! *www. streetcar.photostockplus.com Email: davidmiller@sympatico.ca*

David T. Culver is from Alabama, USA. "My most personal feelings, come from my heart, and sometimes, I would love to think my words touch others in some way or another." For more visit at : http://butterfly36109.tripod.com/shannonpaulk http://moonrising36109.tripod.com *Email: moonrising36109@yahoo.com*

Dawid Wiacek is both a country and a city mouse. He spent a blissful childhood on a farm in Poland, and now continues his adventures living in Brooklyn, NY. Hobbies include traveling, learning new languages and eating candy. He studies at Wesleyan University in Connecticut where, sadly, he is without a dog. *Email: dwiacek@wesleyan.edu*

Debs Higginson: Originally from Bangor, Northern Ireland; painting in oils since her early teens; admires artists like Edward Hopper and Jack Vettriano. Her style ranges from 'thinned' oils to thick impasto effects. The dominant theme within her work is portraiture, but architecture and landscape are also embraced. She prefers to work from photos so she can 'revisit' the painting as many times as is necessary to perfect details. This technique also allows her to paint without the physical presence of the 'sitter', or scene which she is painting. She is currently resident in Swansea, South Wales. *www.debshigginson.com Email : Debs@debshigginson.com*

Dennis Everett Newell is from New York; published in *True Poet Magazine April 2005, Taj Mahal Literary Review June 2005 and Dec 2005, and Harvest of the New Millennium.* . Literature has always been a big part of my life. Poetry for me is a way to express myself and rid my internal demons. The middle name Everett has been passed on through 5 generations originating from a Great Great Grandfather and the Civil War through my Son, who is also a Poet. *Email: Bygd1@aol.com*

Dominique Lecomte took Art courses at the School of Images in Epinal (France), then he went to the USA in 1994, and he specialized in landscapes made with relief printing techniques. He uses photography as a visual travel log. His works do not describe particular places but the ideas related to them.

For more visit at : http://www.lecomtedominique.com Email: lecomtedominique@hotmail.com

Emily A. Reed, Ph.D., creates oil paintings, calligraphy, designs and art photography. She emphasizes landscapes, water scenes, flowers, animals and portraits. She is a top rated artist on ArtWanted.com, frequently having as many as eighty-ninety "Top Tens" on a given day.   Her oil painting "Snowbirds" was chosen by ArtWanted as its "Featured Image" on December 4-5, 2005. http://www.artwanted.com/artist.cfm?artid=16838 Email: ereed@udel.edu

Eric Tessier from Les Lilas, France writes both in French and English; a published author in France, Belgium, USA and India (*Taj Mahal Review.*) Editor of the French literary magazine *La Nef Des Fous*, story editor for *Place Aux Sens* (France) and *Skyline Magazine* (USA.)

Erika Brodie: "Now after years of perfecting and making mistakes, I think that I have become well-known for my crazy abstractions on glass, canvas, and with watercolors. I have many works all over the US and would love to expand and bring more creations into the homes of people in different cultural environments." For more visit at www.artwanted.com/erikalynn *Email: enrique_denver78@hotmail.com*

Floriana Hall (b.1927) Author, Poet, Lyricist from Ohio, USA. Six nonfiction inspirational books, three of them poetry. Many short stories and winning poems published online (check Google). Founded and coordinate The Poet's Nook, a group of local poets who promote the art of poetry, and whose passion is writing poetry. Last year they donated a Poetic Christmas Tree for the benefit of Children's Hospital. This year they will donate money to The Haven of Rest. Floriana is also working on two new books, one to help the medical profession, tentatively titled A TALE OF MENDED HEARTS, and a new poetry book, titled TOUCHING THE HEARTS OF GENERATIONS. This poetry book will include Children's poetry winners along with poems of The Poet's Nook members.

Greg Edwards: "My dad influenced me to expand. I started having out of the body experiences. Once, I felt an infinitely strong wind poor over me, releasing me from the clay cage and up into the air I went. That was my first flight. I have seen many masters as they greeted me through the third eye, one after another, when I was in prison for drugs at 19. I felt honored in a really big way. They were from many different cultures and times. I have had multitudes of spiritual experiences, which prompted me to explore many religious aspects. A common synergy became apparent to me as a universal thread in spiritual experiences... When my only child died I went into deep drug induced psychosis in an insane attempt to escape. Then because I complained to a doctor about anxiety and explained a small bit about some of my "abnormal" experiences, I was forced to take major tranquilizers under a null diagnosis… Life, to me, is more about the journey than destination. And like Art Garfunkle said in one of his songs: "Isn't it a lovely ride>>>the secret of life is enjoying the passage of time>>>There ain't nothing to it. All you do is do it>>><< Einstein said we could never get it all figured out>>>but while we're on our way down>>>we might as well enjoy the ride>>." so, I took the long road to what faith means to me. And, I get your point: it is kind of abstract." E-Mail: catazone2020@yahoo.com

Greg VandeVisser lives and works on Maryland's Eastern Shore. His

concentration in art is primarily in painting and found object constructions. He has a BA in visual communication and works in the design and advertising field. Email: greg@vandevisser.com

Jan Kolling (b. 1962) in the City of Haarlem, The Netherlands; became a professional Artist in 1982; one man exhibitions and group showings all over Europe (1984 - 2005); Artwork in several private collections and Museums in the Netherlands, Belgium and Germany. *E-Mail: jankolling@hetnet.nl*

Jan Oscar Hansen: Collections "Letters from Portugal" "Lunch in Denmark" "A Cherry Tree And A Dog" "Cyberwit Anthologies" and many magazines and poetry sites.

Janet K. Brennan is a poet and author living in Albuquerque, New Mexico. Amongst her most recent publications, she is featured in Doug Hill's "The Power of Prayerful Living," Miracle of the Doves, Rodale Books, 2001, The International Who's Who in Poetry, 2004, Taj Mahal Review, Insights Collection of Contemporary Short Stories, Quill Magazine, April, 2005, Common Swords Magazine" March, 2005 and is also published in numerous anthologies in the United States, The United Kingdom and India. Janet also is the founder and Chief Editor of "Pearls, Inc, JB Stillwater. *Email: jbstillwater@yahoo.com FAX: 1-805-563-2945*

Jean Ann Fitzhugh has been into Photography for about 9 years and loves to Photograph Local Areas and Beyond. For more visit at : http://www.pbase.com/genieslot/galleries Email: Jean.Fitzhugh@Homecall.co.uk

JEM Wellen, 44, from Holland. "I started to write in English because of the internet. It is like writing song lyrics. I publish them on my website and call them internet lyrics. I like web design and all things graphic." *Email: anjawellen@home.nl*

Jennifer Johnson, UNC-CH graduate, is a native of Hatteras Island, NC.

Photographing the Outer Banks' amazing wildlife and ever-changing scenery has let her turn a feeling of "seeing things differently" into a way to share her view with other people, and help them search for beauty in every day. *www.photosfromtheporch.com Email: hatteras5@earthlink.net*

Jeremy R Meier: Subscribing under the ubiquitous title of "designer," Jeremy Meier's artistic profile expands upon several realms of influences and typologies. Graduated upon the educational foundation of architecture, Jeremy's creative vision takes its form through mediums such as photography, web design, architecture, graphics, and industrial design. *Email: meierxl@gmail.com*

Jerry Bradley is Dean of Graduate Studies and Associate Vice President for Research at Lamar University. He is the author of four books including *The Movement: British Poets of the 1950s* (criticism, Twayne) and *Simple Versions of Disaster* (poetry, University of North Texas Press), which was commended by the *Dictionary of Literary Biography*. A member of the Texas Institute of Letters, Bradley was chosen as the 2000 Joe D. Thomas Scholar-Teacher of the Year by the Texas College English Association, and he received the 2005 Frances Hernandez Teacher-Scholar Award by the Conference of College Teachers of English. His poetry has appeared in many literary magazines including *New England Review, American Literary Review, Modern Poetry Studies, Poetry Magazine,* and *Southern Humanities Review.* He is also poetry editor of *Concho River Review* and is past-president of the Texas Association of Creative Writing Teachers and the Southwest/Texas Popular Culture Association.

Jim Corbett is a Canadian expat living in Seongnam, S. Korea with his wife, Sunmi. He teaches English at Kyoungwon University. During the past 16 years, Jim has worked as a language educator in three countries. Besides photography, Jim also enjoys hiking, reading and watching ice hockey. *Email: me@topmail.ca*

Jim Ganley is an alumnus of St. Anselm College and for the past thirteen years has been the director of Gym Ganley Athletic Shapes, a health & wellness consulting practice located in Bow, New Hampshire. Over the years he has coached scores of athletes to championship status in a variety of sports.

As a competitive, drug-free bodybuilder for a decade, Jim won the Mr. New Hampshire title in 1977, was named New Hampshire's Outstanding Bodybuilder Of The Year in 1980, and has competed at the national level, his last competition venture being the 1982 Mr. America Contest. Additionally he has authored two novels, *Winding Up Behind The Eightball* and *Tales From Behind the Eightball*, both of which deal with disillusioned American youth coming of age in the 1960s and '70s. *Email: mrnh77@earthlink.net*

Joseph Ganley is a freshman at Bow High School in the town of Bow, New Hampshire. Only 15 years old, he still holds the record for the mile run which he did in fourth grade in six minutes flat. His gym teacher continues to be amazed that he was able to achieve this while following no formal fitness program. His current passion is music, playing drums in the school marching band, orchestra, and jazz band. For the past several years he has been a virtuoso on blues guitar and can currently be seen on the MTV special <u>Made</u> which presents young, rising rock stars.

Joseph Steven Valencia (b. 1952) has remained a lifelong native of Southern California. His father was Joseph Valencia, Navajo and Cherokee decent and mother, Elidia Valenzuela, Yaqui decent. The first picture he painted was of Christopher Columbus's sailing ships. Watercolor and acrylic are his favorite medium on just about any surface. The colors of his palette are southwestern and influenced by his native desert home. He painted his first mural in grade school a 4'x 8' of the local water company. In 1970 Valencia was recognized as the "Artist of the Year". He was on the Board of Directors for the Victor Valley Museum in California in 1985. He was the art director and a principal of "The Art Tile West" in the 1990s. This is where he established his international reputation for his ceramic tile murals. One of his murals is on permanent display in Petropavlovsk, Kamchatka, Russia. His art and tile work has shown in national and international exhibitions from San Diego, Mexico City, Nairobi to Russia. Valencia loves to paint with his six-year-old granddaughter Haley named after the comet. She is developing her portfolio of art. When Grandfather Valencia tries to assist her with her art she says "Grandpa I love you, but do not touch my work." *Email: joseph_v7@yahoo.com*

Karen Pike (b. 1975) from Los Angeles, CA is ambitious, and her new work reveals a sophisticated awareness of the forces at play. "I feel that my paintings are very specifically influenced by Mondrian's use of segments and color. They stretch beyond their borders so that each painting seems a fragment of a larger cosmos. The work acquires a second, illusory, scale by which the distances between points on the canvas seem measurable in miles." Karen is part of a group of Los Angeles artists that are evolving before our very eyes. Her oeuvre is an impression of styles informed by current and past experiences. *www.artwanted.com/kpike Email: kpikeart@yahoo.com*

Kari Korhonen was born 3.4. 1980 in Joensuu Finland. He has, like most have, drawn all of his short life but it wasn't until the age of 17 when a art teacher walked to him pastels saying "I think you'll love these." Going through surgeries and bullying and some personal issues Kari developed his "darker vision" you can see in his work of Finnish melancholy. Kari has had numerous exhibitions in Finland (Rauma, Pori, Jyväskylä, Turku) and has sold numerous pieces to customers. Known mostly by his sad-styled paintings Kari has created a subculture in his country that is built by the collective pain we all feel no matter what's the cause. *Email: Kari.Korhonen@oras.com*

Karunesh Kumar Agrawal from India has taught in a Post-graduate college of CSJM University; published in *Taj Mahal Review* and *Harvests of New Millennium. www.artwanted.com/cyberwit Email: karunesh1976@yahoo.com*

Kym Lovell lives in Brisbane, Australia. "I work with all different types of media. I have been painting/drawing ever since I can remember. Some of my favourite artists include, Van Gough, Dali, Monet, Candy Jernigan. Through time I have created my own unique style, if would describe most of my pieces as expressive abstract/mixed media." *Email: miss_kym@hotmail.com*

Linda Block studied at the Denver Darkroom, and discovered that photography ignited a passion that seemed a natural fit. Based on her fascination with all things beautiful, in nature and man-made, her photography reflects the simple moments of observation and the delight in discovering more. There is Introspection, the Spirit of Person and Place and a deep respect for all that she encounters. Linda's photos are as lovely and eclectic as her life journey. They are all moments captured in the blink of an eye, a sense of something worth savoring and sharing. As a Feng Shui Practitioner, Holistic Healer and Artist, Linda has a strong sense of the profound effect our environments have on us and feels photography can bring the sacred energies of nature into our home and workspaces. *Ph. 303-877-0142 www.sacred-spaces.net Email: ladydragonfly@sprintmail.com*

L Lindall, a self-taught artist, has been creating art over the past decade. "My vision while I am creating art is to make something beautiful, something emotional, and something which comes to life. I work with a variety of mediums creating many different styles. My styling ranges from realism to impressionistic." *Email: lindalindall@sbcglobal.net*

Lárus G is an Icelandic artist and glassblower. His work ranges from traditional blown glass to installations, collages and sculptures of stone, glass and metal. Living and working in Denmark Lárus´s G´s sculpture "The Traveller" displays a matchstickman; made in blown and handshaped glass and stainless steel, on his way to the world. One can experience more of Lárus´s G´s art at *http://www.hotglass.dk Email: larusg@hotglass.dk*

Louie Levy: "All my life ... I've wanted to write something special, then, when hurting real bad, tears sneaked from my crying heart, and went filling an empty pen with a helping hand My Brooklyn, NY upbringing eventually had me less tolerant of the cold damp weather. Eventually migrating with my family to So, Ca. in 1975. Currently, I'm still enjoying my sunny home living as a single semi-retired, now independent western dude. Hey! Where have all the cowboys and horses gone? I've been writing poetry for seventeen years, since having the insight to discover that...

'Best friends we can be 'me and me',

loneliness was not finding 'me',

Focusing on the wonders of photography is another of my special interests. I'm currently out-reaching for an ageless, kinship camaraderie of poetry/photography oriented individuals to join with in traveling to some proverbial corners of what's left safe on this Earth. Newly discovered experiences that will further fill these pages with adventure, passion and literary treasures. Please E-mail me having similar interests. My personally favored publisher; writings contained in Cyberwit.net, *Explorers, Insights, Taj Mahal Review*, Dec.04, June'05, forthcoming, Dec.'05...., *Harvests of New Millennium, Art and Poetry*. Many years on various forums, e-zines and BBs, Guest spoken for Peace, Love and its creative writing at Simi Valley, Ca Cultural Art Ctr, soon planed at Moorpark Community College, Simi Valley, Ca."E-mail: *louielevy@aol.com* Web: http://www.cornerpoetry.com/poetry/levy_l/levy.html

Marguerite Carstairs, also known as Ladymaggic, is a traveler with a camera in one hand and her laptop in the other. She delights in taking photos and sharing the on her many websites. Marguerite has spent most of her life in Melbourne, Australia and since 1992 has been traveling and teaching Art and studying and learning about different cultures and communities, mostly in the outbacks of Australia and New Zealand, then around the world during vacations. Currently she is teaching English in Korea. *http://M-carstairs.com/travel Email: maggi_carstairs@yahoo.com*

Marie Calow: Born in 1960 to a northern family with Scottish and Irish roots. "My narratives are essentially arrived at through research and experience of places and journeys, there is a strong recyclic quality to some of my work; one piece often giving evolution to the next. I have also made '3-d' objects and I do paint, but my journeys and location work is all photographic or filmic. Time is a large element of my practice therefore movement or a lack of it is often an element in my work. Sometimes there is an educative element in my work I'm told!" *Email: mariecalow@aol.com*

Maureen Audley lives in the north west of England. Her interest is in writing short stories and articles, primarily for pleasure

Michael Estabrook is from MA, USA. "I'm a Marketing Communications Manager for a tiny division of a gigantic billions-of-dollars company, and man, going into an office every day can be excruciating. The stuffy air, the florescent lights are killing me. Thankfully I can retire in 10 or 15 years. But I still think that somehow I've got to get myself on some boat collecting phytoplankton, or into the rich brown hills of Montana searching for TRex bones. Then again maybe I simply should've stayed on Northfield Avenue where I belong and learned to fix cars like my Daddy did."

Mike Howe has been taking photos for a number of years from 1975. "I have begun painting from nature in a meditative creative role, Nature interests me & our role here on earth, I like to paint natural things, & hope that the art shows to us the real beauty of the subject, Gods creation." *Email: michael.howe50@tesco.net*

Mirsad Mehulic last 20 years works as graphic designer and prepress manager in printing & design company, but painting was his passion from university days. Start with oil on glass and canvas, but last 15 years discovers beauty and challenge of watercolors. Last ten years discovering reflections of water, waves and beauty of shores on Adriatic sea and its untouched landscapes. Small fishing boats are his obsession. *Pazinska 30, 10000 Zagreb, CROATIA Tel: ++385 1 3632071 http://www.mehulic-art.com Email: m.mehulic@hi.t-com.hr*

Patricia Fritsche: "The incorporating of sight and feelings I consider myself a photo-poet widely seen on the internet, as I constantly try to explore new perceptions. Enjoy the creativity and exploring of a particular muse since this has been a passion of mine for some time. Combining the dimensions one feels in certain kinds of poetry and the constantly changing perceptions in photography is my passion now." *http://www.piksinthe-digital.nl/index.htm Email: UNDENYING@aol.com*

Patricia Wellingham-Jones, former psychology researcher, writer, editor, lecturer Patricia Wellingham-Jones has recently been published in *Edgz, Ibbetson Street Press, Underground Window, HazMat Review, Taj Mahal Review, Ink&Ashes.* She is a three-time Pushcart Prize nominee. Her newest books are *Belt of Transit* (PWJ Publishing) and *Hormone Stew* (Snark Publishing); also published is *Don't Turn Away: Poems about Breast Cancer. www.wellinghamjones.com Email: pwj@wellinghamjones.com*

Pepita Selles: "Living in the "middle" of Sweden, in a small place called Kungsör, newly named "The Kingdom Kungsör" (kungariket kungsör) Because of ancient time kings love for this beautiful place. My art is maybe a sort of unusual in different ways. My collages/mixed media digital themes. 1) I mix paint acryl with real living flowers.. things. 2) Photos leafs, flowers...... 3)digital freehand painting and computer art, 4)And my art forms is for me now pop art/fantasy and collage reality realism… And as single mum, to my precious teenage boy, 13 years old. (And me 46) Art (reading writing..) have been something we have in common." *http://www.pepitas.741.com Email: flowerhearts@telia.com*

Phil Kunin: "I am 34 years old, live in the Los Angeles Area, I have been involved with photography for about 12 years, I do street photography in the US and abroad, also do allot of photography with Rock and Roll Groups, I have travel led across the United States, Canada, England and France taking photos of unusual scenes and objects. Photography is my passion. I plan on traveling through Europe this summer taking pictures." *Email: calkunin@yahoo.com*

Rebecca L Phillips: "My lifelong experience in the arts, both lively and visual arts, began at the age of five years with the study of classical music and theory at the Philadelphia Conservatory of Music (now the University of the Arts). At the age of twelve years theatre Arts were added at the Children's Repertory Theatre in Philadelphia. Later, I entered the world of the more modern visual arts of video, film, and photography and theatre at Temple University where I received a Bachelor of Science degree in 1972, graduating with two majors (communications and theatre) and two minors (journalism and psychology).completed. In 1994, with the advent of Apple's Power

MacIntosh desktop computers, I began working in training myself in Computer Generated Imagery. By 1999, my experimentation with using original fractals as material presets in 3D computer imagery began in earnest, as I healed from a major stroke in my brain. … the inner process of this artist to produce the outer creative work remains the same from artform to artform. Some of the major aspects of that process I believe to be, insight, focus, discipline, and knowing when to stop!" *www.ArtWanted.com/Fractal3DArt Email: eppesart1@yahoo.com*

Robert L. Bills from FL, USA: "I am an old-young wildlife Photographer. My wife and I never fail to seek out new wildlife visions wherever we go. From Florida where these shots were taken to Alaska where we found an abundance of subjects... By the way, I am 75 years young which goes to prove it is never too late to start anything." *Email: rbills@cfl.rr.com*

Robin M Buehler is a journalist in southern NJ, USA. Her work has appeared in both print and online publications. She has also exhibited her photographs including receiving honors for some of her pictures. *Email: RBueh5672@aol.com*

Robert M. Wilson: From the Nameless to a name, Robert M. Wilson came. Born by the Yangzi Jiang, now the U.S. Rio Grande he rows. Still riding rapids, mathematics navigator is his game Until the Great River back to the Unknown Ocean flows.

Roger Cummiskey is a Dublin Watercolourist, living between Ireland and southern Spain. He has developed a unique individual style and specializes in paintings that take their themes and titles from the wanderings and writings of James Joyce, Samuel Beckett, Miguel de Cervantes and other Literary and Historical personalities. He is a recognised Joycean artist. Roger's unique style and individual talent have won him worldwide acclaim. His paintings have been exhibited in China, UK, USA, Sweden, Spain, France, Australia, Finland and Italy as well as in many national shows in Ireland. Roger has represented Ireland at the Florence Biennale and also at International art exhibitions in London, Stockholm and New York. *www.RogerCummiskey.com www.aia-group.net Email: artroger@gmail.com Tel: +34 952 592 652 +34 666 7826 42*

Sam Stearman moved to Hong Kong in 2003 from San Diego CA. Since relocating, he has been an active traveler and photographer, a member of PSA and a General Committee member of FAPA – Hong Kong & Macau Chapter. His work "Sam's Exotic Travels" can be found on the web at *www.samsays.com* Email: samsays@gmail.com

Sandra Busby is an international award-winning photographer who has been traveling and shooting in Europe for more than ten years. To her wealth of images of Paris and Italy, especially Florence and Venice, she adds spectacular shots of Prague, Spain, and Istanbul which may be seen on her *www.sandrabusbyphotography.com Email: busbysandra@yahoo.com*

Shari Travison is an amateur photographer and artist currently residing in the Pacific Northwest. She enjoys photographing nature, animals and man-made objects (e.g., architecture & sculptures). Some of her photos are used as a basis for creating both traditional and digital art. *Email: photos@travison.com*

Shirley Bolstok was born and lives in Denver, Colorado in the United States. "I have been writing since I was 10 years old. My parents were from Europe, my mother is still living and I have one sister. I have had poetry published in numerous books, journals, magazines, online magazines and newspapers over the years and am internationally published. I am extremely proud to be featured in an anthology such as this one. This is a collection of some of my older poetry mixed with some new ones." *Email: SBolstok@vgic.com Fax: 303-831-5295*

Steven P. Love: A small business owner living in Arizona USA. "I make my living primarily by delivering TVs and selling Solar Power Systems but I have also included my talents as an artist in my business portfolio. At my website, www.deepdesertent.com, you will also see that I sell my artwork as well as photographs from my travels through Arizona. I also offer Photographic enhancement and photo manipulation services." *Email: sales@deepdesertent.com Tel. 623-680-5692.*

Tabitha L. Borges is influenced by Michael Parkes, Claude Monet and other surrealistic artists. "…but my biggest influence as a photographer/artist is my grandfather, recently deceased professional photographer, Robert Thompson. At age eight, he bought me my first camera and spent countless hours encouraging my art. Because of his encouragement, I have a great way to spend time, drawing, painting, and taking photos of my favorite subjects people and nature. Because of my photography and the arts I have learned that an artist speaks not only to people, they speak for them. Art is a weapon against ignorance and hatred and an agent of public awareness. Art opens new doors for learning, understanding and peace among people and nations." *www.artwanted.com/rose2823 Email: jntborges@comcast.net*

Tatiana Pahlen was born, raised, and completed University in Moscow, Russia; fascinated by Russian literature. "Since my arrival in New York in '86, I translated some of my efforts, then started writing poetry directly in English, a language I respect and worship for its beauty. Aside of the many poems I wrote, I dab also in non-fiction and cartoons for my pleasure. Currently I'm working on my first poetry book, called "Poetry and Eye"." *Email: tatianyc@worldnet.att.net*

Tazda Lawson: "First of all I'm a poorly published artist.... I have recently started painting and carving wooden eggs. I enjoy Illustration more.... with sequential art (comic book art) coming in a close second. My education in art has been a long and difficult one...... I'm a sarcastic artist but not to be confused with a smart mouth." *Email: stavart03@yahoo.com*

Trisha Allard (b. 1975) "I am currently a stay at home mother, and my children are and always be top priority in my life. I have been an amateur photographer for 3 years now and love what I do. When ever I get the chance to travel, I usually see the trip through my photo lens. I enjoy photography and the creativeness it has added to my life." *Email: trixieor@yahoo.com*

Yvonne Sparkes: "Born in Feb. 1940 at Barkingside, Essex, England. I left England after the war in April 1948 to take up residence in Long Island, New York, U.S.A. I completed my education and returned to England in September 1958. I married and had two sons Jon and David. David is married now to Gayle, and I have three beautiful grandchildren Daniel, Emma and Rebecca. I worked until my divorce at a Livestock Research Centre, and after my divorce for 32 years until my retirement in a local Chelmsford Hospital. 18 of those years working as a nurse on a Mental Health Assessment Unit for the over 69's. I retired in 2000 from full time nursing. I have written poetry for a number of years and was encouraged to write at a very early age by my American schoolteachers. I have made many friends worldwide through the Internet where my poetry is placed on various sites of poetry. I have received much happiness from receiving e-mails from people throughout the world telling me how he or she likes my poetry. I was voted Poet Of The Year, 2003 by a group of Poets on a very fine site called "Poetry For Thought". The founder lives in Hawaii and has become a good friend. Many of my poems have been published in magazines, journals, anthologies, Newspapers in Britain, U.S.A, Australia, Canada, Israel, Germany, and India." *Email: y.sparkes@btinternet.com*

ABOUT THE EDITOR

Dr. Santosh Kumar (b. 1946)

is a poet, short-story writer and an editor
from UP India; Head of the English Department in
A.D. College, Allahabad; D.Phil in English; several
awards; poems published in many anthologies; Chief Editor
of an international literary journal *Taj Mahal Review*. He has
also edited fifteen World Poetry Anthologies, and four books
of World's Great Short Stories. He is also the author of a
new collection of poems entitled *Helicon* (Cyberwit,
2006, India, ISBN 81-901366-8-2).